HOW TO PROMOTE YOUR BUSINESS & INCREASE SALES

An Excellent Sales Promotion & Social Media Marketing Book for Business Owners & Managers.

Professor Andy, MBA Trained Specialist

A2 Best Seller Publishers

Softcover ISBN: 979-8-9871746-0-9

Hardcover ISBN: 979-8-9871746-2-3

EBook ISBN: 979-8-9871746-1-6

Audio Book ISBN: 979-8-9871746-3-0

2nd Edition

A2 Best Seller Publishers

Printed in the United States of America

Contents

Dedication · 1

1. Introduction · 3
2. Social Media Platforms · 7
3. Branding & Brand Awareness · 17
4. Online Promotions & Advertising · 31
5. 21 Free & Low-Cost Advertising · 37
6. Holidays Sales & Grand Openings · 41
7. Targeted Emails & Email Newsletters · 55
8. Business Cards, Flyers & Brochures · 59
9. Network & Collaborate with others · 63
10. Direct Mail Marketing · 73
11. Radio & Television Advertising · 79
12. Telephone & Sales Reps · 83
13. Newspapers & Print Advertising · 87
14. Bid Lists & Government Contracts · 91
15. Indoor & Outdoor Advertising Signs · 95

16. 68 Ways to Obtain Customers — 101

17. 350 Ways to Promote Books/Courses — 131
   Linkedin
   Google Ads
   Twitter for Authors
   Facebook Author Page
   Facebook Ads
   Instagram Promotions
   Landing Page Strategies
   Influencer Marketing
   Webinar
   Forum Marketing
   Selling to Book Stores
   Book Event
   Email Newsletter
   Book/Product Reviews
   Free Book Promotion Sites
   Paid Book Promotion Sites
   Press Release
   Goodreads
   Affiliate Marketing

18. To All Our Valued Readers — 202

19. Other Services We Provide — 203

20. Index — 205

Dedication

Greetings

WE ARE DEDICATING THIS book to all the Healthcare Professionals, doctors, nurses, and everyone else, who helped save lives during the COVID-19 pandemic.

We say "Thank you" for your demanding work and dedication. Many of these healthcare professionals are also business owners in various industries besides their regular full-time career work.

The COVID-19 Pandemic of 2020 and 2021 not only resulted in economic lockdowns and hospitalizations worldwide, but millions of people died from it, according to the Centers for Disease Control (CDC). Thanks to the scientists and researchers who invented the vaccines and effective treatments to bring the pandemic under control.

During the lockdown, people had plenty of free time, and many started online businesses using various platforms.

Although many existing businesses were temporarily closed, many more quickly took advantage of the internet and online social media platforms. As a result, traditional companies could survive by increasing their online presence, engaging their audiences, and generating sales. This book can help such business owners retain and attract new customers.

Who is this book for?

We hope this 2nd edition of: "How to Promote your Business & Increase Sales" can be of value to business owners, managers, and anyone else, who wants to own a business in 2023 and beyond.

Thank you for your time and consideration. Have a wonderful day.

Chapter One

Introduction

Welcome

FRESH OUT OF BRYANT College (now Bryant University}, in Smithfield, Rhode Island, a young graduate with a Master's degree in Business Administration (MBA) authored the first edition of this book, "How To Promote Your Business & Increase Sales," several years ago.

At that time, the writer had no access to an affordable or readily available computer, so he typed the book on a word processor. He manually copied and pasted the manuscripts one page at a time, front and back, to 5.5 inches by 8.5-inch cards and transported them to a local printer.

Fast forward to 2022, computers are now readily available, and books are available in different formats such as; online, print, digital, and audiobooks.

The internet and social media have become very popular and powerful with the growing use of artificial intelligence (AI), the availability of cloud storage, social platforms, email platforms, online search engines, and influencers with millions of followers.

These are a result of the below-listed technological innovations:

1983 Introduction of TCP/IP (transmission control protocol/Internet Protocol)

1984 Introduction of DNS (Domain Name Servers)

1987 Introduction of The Internet

1989 Introduction of The World Wide Web (www.)

1991 Introduction of MP3

1995 Introduction of SSL(Secure Socket Layer) for secure financial transactions

1996 Introduction of Hotmail

1998 Introduction of Google search engine for finding information online

1983 Introduction of Myspace Social media platform

2004 Introduction of Facebook

2005 Introduction of YouTube and video sharing

2006 Introduction of Twitter

2007 Introduction of the iPhone

2008 An increase in the use of the internet and social media platforms.

Presently, Google is the world's largest and most popular search engine. Other large and popular social media platforms include YouTube, Facebook, Instagram, Snapchat, LinkedIn, Twitter, and more.

This book includes online, offline, and social media promotional ideas, thanks to the above technological advancements.

Choosing one or two great ideas from this book is all it takes to start the process of promoting your business and increasing sales. You do not need to implement the hundreds of ideas presented in this book at once to see results.

We suggest that when you get a chance to read this book, write down just two simple ideas and implement them in the next 30 days. After that, select another two ideas you can expand on in the following 30 days.

Before you realize it, you are building a reputable brand and commanding customers' attention. Online, offline, and social media sales promotions are a gradual process that pays off through consistency and patience.

As additional bonuses, to help entrepreneurs to start promoting their businesses quicker, we have included some of our premium and valuable resources in the following chapters:

Chapter Five presents; 21 free or low-cost online classified advertising sites.

Chapter Sixteen presents; 68 ways to obtain and retain customers.

Chapter Seventeen presents; 350 Ways To Promote Books & Courses.

Our goals in this book are to over-deliver by enabling businesses to increase awareness of their brands, reach their target markets and increase sales.

We wish you many satisfied customers and great success.

Chapter Two

Social Media Platforms

The Internet

T HE INTERNET, ALSO KNOWN as the World Wide Web (www), is an extensive system consisting of several computer networks communicating worldwide by land, sea, air, and space.

The internet and social media have much to do with selling your products and services. Social media can keep businesses up to date with market trends by informing them of customers' shopping habits and how to join in and capture market share.

Social Media

Social media is where people and businesses go online to share information, interact with a worldwide audience, shop, trade, and communicate, through various Platforms.

People, businesses, governments, and organizations use social media to share information, learn, conduct research, interact, promote, market, educate, entertain, and connect with people online.

There are many platforms in social media, such as websites, blogs, micro-blogs, social networking sites, photo-sharing sites, instant messaging, group text messages on cellular phones, video-sharing sites, podcasts, widgets, virtual meetings, and more.

Some reliable ways to connect with your target clients are on the internet and social media. However, getting to your clients can be challenging, depending on the quality of your content. Your content on social media platforms and the internet can help increase your audience.

Online shopping has increased worldwide, generating billions of dollars in sales annually, due to the popularity of the internet and social media. It can help grow your brand, obtain valuable insights, and engage with prospects or customers.

Here is an example of how an established, big retail company, with multiple store locations, is achieving tremendous success in both online and offline sales.

Staples

Ever wondered why some large successful companies, such as Staples (the Office Superstore) call their salespeople "associates", rather than "salespeople"?

Answer: These people not only assist in sales but also provide excellent customer service by engaging, assisting, and interacting with customers.

They greet customers, assist with locating items, and if the things are not in stock, they assist in placing online orders for delivery to the customers.

These associates are essential to the company's success, and their services directly affect customer satisfaction and loyalty. Many companies give their associates monthly or quarterly awards.

We have observed similar levels of excellent customer service at other retailers such as Apple Stores, Office Depot, and Target Stores.

As a result of this customer-oriented approach to sales, these companies have many happy and loyal customers.

While several companies have successfully transitioned to online sales, some other large retailers are slow to adapt and are closing many stores, due to increased online competition.

Create a website

A website lets customers contact you quickly and learn more about your products and services. You can help validate your credibility and establish trust through social media platforms, blogs, and your website. Many first-time visitors to your website want to learn more about you and the values of your business.

A website helps to create a great first impression for potential clients. A client can find you online, go to your website, make a purchase, and receive either an instant download of a digital product or a shipment to an address for a physical product.

Invest in a high-quality website that is easily accessible to everyone worldwide.

Blogs

Many businesses include a blog in a section of their websites to explain and present current and ongoing information of interest to an audience.

A blog consists of a header, main content area, or the body, a sidebar that contains a call-to-action such as "register for a free newsletter," "register to win," "register for our free webinar," and a footer that contains links to your website or other posts.

Businesses can use blogs to promote an event, disseminate information, build a brand and engage with the audience.

A blog can be for personal or business use and helps drive traffic to your website. Social media and the posting of articles on blogs, can help you reach your target audience.

The contents of a blog must be of high quality and provide value. Unlike websites, blogs need regular updates to stay current, and readers can post comments.

Bloggers can generate income on their blogs by selling ad space, or digital items such as eBooks or software. They also can promote affiliate links and sell subscriptions.

Some software for creating Blogs include:

Wordpress.com

Wordpresss.org

Tumblr,

Squarespace

Blogger.com.

Podcast

A recording of an event distributed online on various platforms is called a podcast. Some examples of podcasts are recordings of radio programs, interviews, news commentaries, panel discussions, and digital narrations.

Users can subscribe to podcasts.

Businesses use podcasts to share knowledge and get feedback from their audiences.

Promotions on Social Media

For example, during the launch of a toddler food products company, its sales did not meet expectations. To increase sales, the company created an online promotional campaign. It advertised on Instagram Ads every night at 9:00 pm when its target audience was most likely to be online. Within a week, sales increased significantly.

Here are some reminders:

• Keep your target client in mind when creating content and use any information you have on them to make successful posts or run an ad.

• Social media platforms today have advertising tools that can help you zero in on your target client and place your ads before them for high conversion rates.

• Real conversations with your social media following are a great way to collect feedback and create a relationship with your customers, increasing retention rates.

How to Actively participate in Online Forums

Online forums are where your target audience congregates, communicates, and engages in various online activities. Online forums create a space for customers to ask questions, debate, share knowledge, and discuss topics of common interest. Often, new ideas are born from these forums.

They are a powerful source of customer feedback, meaning businesses can get valuable insight at a minimal cost.

Being part of an online forum allows businesses to design products and services that genuinely serve customers' needs. You can collect information in online forums that would otherwise take more time to gather.

Businesses can correct issues or adopt new practices based on customer feedback without involving a support agent. It also empowers customers by encouraging them to share first-hand experiences and making solving problems with a product or service easier.

Add Value to your Product or Service

For example, customers are more likely to buy dinnerware sets with free silverware.

Value-added products and services are a great way to attract customers and maintain them. You can add value to your products or services by:

• Offering significantly higher professionalism and value than your competitors.

• Creating desirable packages at different price levels

• Adding different levels of service for different clients.

• Creating a frequent buyer program to reward loyal customers. For example, many airlines have a frequent flyer program where customers get additional benefits and incentives.

Customer Reviews

Most consumers admit to looking at reviews before purchasing to avoid losses.

Positive reviews encourage your audience to make a purchase. Here is how you can get reviews for your product or service:

• Stay active and post comments on the platforms where your customers are most likely to be because being social and accessible is the best way to get reviews. Make it easy for customers to reach out to you with questions, concerns, or comments.

• Contact customers who leave great reviews and ask permission to share their feedback on channels.

• Contact customers who leave negative reviews and find out how you can best meet their needs in the future. It shows that you are genuinely trying to find solutions and maintain customer satisfaction.

• Give your customers a good reason to leave a positive review by exceeding their expectations.

• Contact a professional marketer for more details and to assist you in creating a strategy.

Search Engine Optimization (SEO)

SEO makes your business more visible in search engines. There are millions of coffee shops advertising their business online. If, for example, you want to find a coffee shop in Queens where you can do some work on your computer and hold a business meeting, you could search for "coffee shop in Queens with free Wi-Fi", using your preferred search engine, such as Google.

Coffee shops that use SEO to reach people like you will pop up, and you can choose the best option that is most convenient. Advertising your brand on search engines can help your business grow.

Search Engine Optimization with the appropriate keywords increases the number of searches for your brand. More online searches can lead to more visitors, and more visitors can lead to more prospects or leads for potential sales.

An optimized SEO increases the chances of your brand appearing high on the search engine's results. To maximize your digital presence, you need a branded website that uses search engine optimization to make it more visible.

It is easier for customers to find your products and services if your brand appears at the top of search results. It also gives credibility to your business.

Influencer Marketing

Influencer marketing is when someone with social media influence, with a large following such as a celebrity, endorses and promotes a brand, product, or service to a target audience.

The influencer promotes a brand to improve brand awareness and gets paid a fee or other incentives.

Businesses benefit from the promotional efforts of influencers through increased sales leads and audience engagement.

Collaborating with influencers gives your business expert social media insight, and exposure to millions of followers.

The Federal Trade Commission (FTC) requires advertisers, marketers, and influencers to disclose publicly any paid content or post. The words "sponsored" can usually be seen in such content.

Marketers should designate paid posts with words such as sponsored ads, promoted, or paid partnerships.

Chapter Three

Branding & Brand Awareness

F OCUS ON HIGH-QUALITY BRANDS & Excellent Customer Service

Do customers recognize and remember your brand? A loyal client base will be familiar with your logo, messaging, and products.

Brand awareness is building name recognition for your product or service. It signifies how people and other businesses know and recognize what your brand provides.

Brand awareness also refers to how aware and informed people are, of your business and what it offers. When you want your customers to understand, recall, and become comfortable with your business, you can invest in brand awareness through active marketing and promotions.

How To Build Your Brand

You can build your brand into a reliable and consistent business with many happy customers. Good branding makes your brand more relatable, easy to remember, and accessible to your client base.

Companies build brand awareness in several ways: creating content, adding comments to other people's social media posts, advertising, participating in sales promotional events, creating an online presence, participating in online group discussions, and educating the public about what a business does.

A well-known brand often leads to more traffic and more sales.

For example, if you are hungry and unsure what specific food to eat, you can go to your favorite all-you-can-eat restaurant and choose from various menu items. If you want to buy office furniture and supplies for your business, it is easy to think of nearby superstores offering low prices and quality products.

How To Measure Brand Awareness

You can measure brand awareness by analyzing your traffic, sales volume, reviews, and comments on social media.

How To Increase Brand Awareness

You can increase brand awareness by putting your business in front of potential customers. Develop a plan to strategically place your ads in blogs, social media platforms, TV, podcasts, and search engines.

Benefits of a Strong Brand

A well-known brand increases customer loyalty and attracts new customers, especially if the brand is unique.

A strong brand usually means a successful business with a high monetary value. You can build your brand by establishing a robust and loyal client base that can help turn it into a household name.

A good brand relates to its target clientele, ensuring that customers know your story and that it resonates with their values. With a consistent and value-based system, you can build a brand that grows with time.

Market Yourself and Brand Identity

Brand identity familiarizes your customers with who you are and what you do.

Your brand should be easily recognizable by your client base for the reliability and high-quality services or products you provide. You can market yourself and your brand by establishing, developing, and managing your social media presence.

As businesses become more sophisticated, leveraging yourself and your brand and aligning it with a product, service, or institutional brand is a profit-generating strategy. It is an excellent strategy for your business because people want to interact with actual humans.

Building a brand around your personality and using this brand together with your corporate brand ensures that you put a face behind your ideas. It is a great way to assure your customers of quality and reliability.

Benefits of Satisfied Customers

Happy Customers can recommend your brand to others because they know it and have used it.

Also, individuals can represent a company's brand to their audience.

When a company offers incentives to such people, they may be willing to go out and help raise awareness of your brand. They can do so because they know your brand.

Others, such as affiliate marketers, usually receive commissions from the company for sales. Affiliates typically have affiliate links that they share with their network.

Importance of a Business Logo

Your business logo is also a significant part of your brand.

They convey your brand's character and identity, so it is essential to ensure that your logo fits your brand's vision.

Know Who Your Customers are

Take an in-depth look at your product or service, analyze its benefits, set a marketing budget, and develop a strategy to promote your business and increase sales effectively.

Your analysis will require answering simple questions such as: What business are you operating? What product/service do you have to offer? How does your product or service compare with that of your competitors? Who are your customers?

You can better understand your market strategy by answering the above questions.

Provide Excellent Customer Service

Companies that provide excellent customer service thrive, whether online or offline. Companies offer customer service in how they communicate, interact, and assist customers in all transactions regarding their companies. Good customer service promotes customer retention and helps to increase sales. Poor customer service makes the customer avoid your business and search for your nearest competitors.

In both online and offline transactions, make it easy for customers to shop as well as to return an item.

Excellent customer service gives your business a good reputation because your customers are usually satisfied. Fulfilling your customers' expectations leads to growth by attracting new customers and retaining old ones. It is the front-line impression that your customers get in response to their needs. Invest in customer service as your business grows.

There is a need for your business to follow up on both positive and negative feedback. It is a great idea to ensure that customer service is a priority in all aspects of your business.

Focus on providing High-Quality Products and Services

Delivering high-quality products and services is essential for success. Your business needs strong leadership, a system that keeps everything on track, and a culture of improvement to deliver high-quality products and services.

In the long run, quality management enhances your business' brand and reputation and protects it against risks while increasing efficiency.

Create Excitement & Demand

You can create a need for your brand by:

• Producing stellar content that is informative and unforgettable.

• Sharing reviews on your social media platforms.

• Giving new customers discounts and incentives to persuade them to try something new. They will likely be inclined to purchase from you again.

• Creating an exclusive club that gives your customers special perks so that they can become part of a community that makes them feel appreciated.

Creating a demand for your business attracts new customers and encourages existing clients to remain loyal.

Importance of Writing Valuable Content

Valuable content persuades your target audience to trust your brand. Audiences are discerning with expectations of relevant and useful content.

Content marketing allows businesses to build authority. Create content that has valuable information about your brand, by focusing on its benefits, and value.

For example, some dentists remind their clients to floss before brushing through printed materials, social media, and online websites/blogs.

They then follow up by giving away free floss, toothbrushes, and toothpaste.

These dentists provide valuable content to help consumers protect their teeth and gums, while providing answers and solutions, hoping to encourage members of the audience to make appointments for dental services.

Likewise, a chef could share the recipe for cooking a chicken soup, or a website designer could share content about what makes a good, responsive website.

The goal of the content is to provide valuable information to consumers and to promote your brand with the hope of getting some sales.

Importance of attention-getting Headline & Description

Headlines and descriptions of your products and services enhance every other marketing strategy. Always try to create attention-getting headlines and product descriptions to make a great first impression.

For example, some entrepreneurs opened a Shopify shop to sell graphic t-shirts. When setting up the shop, they wrote a description, and the prices were friendly, but the returns were not profitable. After evaluation and research, they realized that writing a detailed product description that is SEO focused with relevant and trending keywords attracted more customers to Shopify, which helped them to make sales.

An attention-grabbing headline and product description help your audience to get an idea of what they should expect, and if it matches the reviews, it will convince them to buy what you sell. Consistent research will help you understand what your customers want, and you can tailor your content to attract them to your business.

Write or add Comments to related Articles or online Blogs

Most businesses have a social presence and engage with their audience on various platforms. Visitors can post comments, ask questions, and communicate with others. They can also provide expert advice and opinions to similar online articles and blogs. You can visit these sites and build relationships with potential clients.

Engaging your clients with valuable content and responding to their needs, builds trust and encourages people to visit your online site or business.

How Businesses Adapted to the COVID-19 Pandemic

The Covid-19 pandemic of 2020 affected prices, consumer behavior, and shopping patterns. Many consumers and businesses were quick to adapt to such changes.

When the pandemic started, people went into panic mode, buying needed household and food items until store shelves became empty in several locations.

What followed during the shutdown was a challenging situation for businesses. Employees were unavailable, production of goods was slow due to production delays, and for the unsold stock, companies had to find ways to sell them.

Many employees lost their jobs, and those employed worked remotely from home. The only exception was essential workers such as healthcare professionals, doctors, nurses, and law enforcement.

Many businesses successfully use the internet and social media to sell online. They are making their products and services available online, and anyone from across the globe with an internet connection can connect or shop.

Supply chain disruptions significantly affected the price of production and transportation as consumer prices went up temporarily. However, despite inflation, there are still significant online sales.

Supply and demand affect the decision-making process of any business that wants to make a profit. Businesses always benefit when they supply a product or service that has a high demand.

For example, in 2020, at the onset of the pandemic, there was a high demand for face masks and supply was low, making prices to go up.

Prices went up very high for several months due to shortages, low supply, and high demand. However, prices went down as supply increased, and demand decreased as the pandemic subsided in 2021.

How To Use This Book for Direct Promotions &
Not Business-As-Usual

Some young adults in 2022 are becoming
overnight successes, sensational celebrities, and
doing great things their parents could not
dream of in the 1980s. Your possibilities are
endless, thanks to the internet and social media.

As a result of these above-mentioned online
trends and the desire to create an impact in
people's lives, we feel this book can be helpful
to businesses, small, medium, and large.

We are presenting, with great honor and respect
to our readers, several small pieces of information that are easy to remember and implement
throughout this book.

It is always a great idea to show up on time, be
visible and position yourself as a market leader.

As a reminder of the past, we believe that playing your own trumpet, at the appropriate place
and time, can be great for any business.

Here are seven suggestions as to how businesses
and people can use this book, "How To Promote
Your Business & Increase Sales," to promote
brand awareness:

1. Give as Gifts to Others

We encourage you to give this book as a gift
to family, friends, and co-workers. It could be
helpful to them when they least expect it.

2. Sell Without Selling

Companies can acquire new businesses without selling by doing something natural and simple. They can give away free copies of this book to their business clients, prospective leads, and website visitors.

It shows that you want your business clients to be very successful and could result in more purchases from you. It also shows that you care and seek your business customers' best interests.

3. Giveaways at Business Events

It could also be an excellent gift to business managers and professionals who register for trade shows, meetings, events, and online presentations.

4. Retailers Can Give to Business Customers

Large retailers can build customer loyalty, retention, goodwill, and brand awareness by giving their business clients and customers a copy of this book with their brand name and logo, printed on the bottom cover, below the book's title. Branded copies of this book are available from the publisher.

5. A Sales Tool for New Business Clients

Service businesses such as Accountants, Bookkeepers, Attorneys, Business Consultants, Office Products Suppliers, and Social Media Influencers can benefit by giving valuable giveaways to their business customers, with their names and logos printed on them by the book's publisher.

Giving business customers free copies of a twenty-dollar business book can lead to additional sales of hundreds or thousands of dollars of business products, furniture, computers, copy machines, and office supplies.

6. Branding with Your Business Name & Logo

Branding is available (directly from the publisher) with your business name and logo on this book's front cover, below the title.

Branding reminds business customers of your brand when they are ready to purchase a high-ticket item.

7. Up to 50% Volume Discount is Available

The publisher is offering up to 50% off, on volume purchases of 200 books or more, from any business, professional, or fundraising organization.

For Email Information on quantity discounts or branding, contact the publisher at the email address provided at the end of this book.

Unknown BRAND?
CREATE
BRAND
AWARENESS?

Chapter Four

Online Promotions & Advertising

BUSINESSES SHOULD CONSTANTLY TRY to meet or exceed their customers' expectations.

Delivering high-quality products and services requires a business to understand who the customers are and their needs. It is also essential to involve other people, such as your staff and professionals, in your sales promotions.

Your business needs strong leadership, a system that keeps everything on track, and a culture of improvement to deliver high-quality products and services. Overall, quality maintenance enhances your business' brand and reputation and protects it against risks.

Valuable content in promotional materials should target the right people. For businesses, promotional advertising materials need to be of high quality. This attention to detail draws and captures customers' attention, making them loyal to your brand.

Online content also needs to be tailored to a specific audience. Every audience appreciates valuable content where people can learn something new and get tips to improve their lives.

When businesses add value to their content, clients appreciate the thoughtfulness and thank the company by buying and referring them to their friends, family, and acquaintances.

Investing time and resources to add value to your business is always worthwhile.

Online and Digital Advertising

Digital marketing is advertising your content, images, videos, and podcasts online and on social media platforms. Such ads appear on search engines, display advertising, email marketing, mobile ads, text messaging, and native advertising.

Businesses use online advertising to sell their products and services. It is also possible to advertise locally on Google Maps and Yelp.

A digital marketing strategist could advertise on appropriate advertising networks to gain momentum within new markets.

Online and digital advertising requires businesses to identify the best method to promote their campaigns for maximum conversion.

Online and digital advertising allows businesses to track campaigns and know when specific keywords, times, and target groups are no longer working and when they are performing best.

When you want to put your business before people who need your services, consider their behaviors and create ads that are most likely to impress them.

Native Advertising is sponsored or paid ads on social media platforms, and news websites. They sometimes look like content marketing but are paid ads, such as videos appearing before, during, or after a regular video.

Advertising on mobile networks requires a network that offers targeted mobile advertising. You can devise a strategy and test a smaller number to see which one works best.

Facebook and how to promote on it

Facebook is one of the largest networks in the world. Businesses can acquire loyal customers and expand their reach to an international market.

Facebook has billions of users worldwide. With these many people on the platform, businesses can advertise on social media platforms and reach their preferred audience through Facebook feeds, business pages, groups, and the Facebook marketplace.

Businesses use Facebook to communicate with consumers, advertise, and promote their products and services to targeted audiences.

YouTube and how to promote on it

YouTube has billions of users globally. You promote your brand as follows:

· Pay influencers with thousands of YouTube subscribers can help promote your brand to their audience.

· Create videos and post them on YouTube. Respond to comments and commonly asked questions about your brand.

· Use YouTube Live streams to engage with your audience and discuss your products and services.

· Use YouTube to run your ads and target audiences worldwide or locally.

LinkedIn and how to promote on it

LinkedIn is a popular social media site for many businesses and professional people.

Consider writing articles on LinkedIn.

When you hear LinkedIn, the first thing that comes to mind is applying for jobs. Businesses, however, can use LinkedIn as a marketing platform and make sales through recommendations and paid advertising.

Using paid advertising, a business that sells notebooks, Journals, and diaries can use LinkedIn to ensure that they get sales by being on top of the list when someone searches for the journal, notebooks, and similar items on LinkedIn.

Businesses can also use recommendations to send messages to their network and other LinkedIn users.

Twitter and how to promote on it

Twitter is a tool for business growth, brand awareness, and spreading the news about your business. A company like Hubspot, uses Twitter to increase brand awareness, boost conversion, and engage its audience. Within a few minutes, your content on Twitter can reach millions of people.

Using a Twitter moment to markct your products or services can help. Many businesses successfully use trending topics on Twitter to reach their target audience.

Instagram and how to promote on it

Instagram provides a platform for promoting your products or services. Instagram has a large audience where a potential target market exists, and getting your product or service before them will convince them to buy.

Evans, a sculptural artist, relies on his social media platforms to make about 80% of his money. He found he could increase sales by promoting his art through Instagram ads. Interestingly, many leads and requests after the Instagram ads are new.

eBay and how to promote on it

eBay helps businesses and individuals open new markets abroad and at home.

The company provides sales tools like promotions manager and promoted listings standard, which helps your products to get more visibility.

· Promotions manager helps account owners to offer codeless coupons for discounts.

· The advanced and standard promotional listings can help your products stand out from the competition and promote sales.

Google Ads and how to promote on it

Businesses and individuals advertise on Google Ads to their target markets to create awareness, leads, and possible sales.

When people click on an ad, a link directs them to a website, blog, or landing page with a call to action as to what to do next.

Ads can go live and start running in approximately forty-eight hours upon ad approval and payment arrangements.

The amount you pay accumulates each time a customer clicks on your ad. and is called pay-per-click.

Businesses can segment their ads by choosing which location they want them to appear and the length of time they wish to run the ads.

Chapter Five

21 Free & Low-Cost Advertising

HERE ARE SOME ONLINE business listing and sales promotion sites you can use to promote your business

Online business directories are the modern-day Yellow Pages for businesses, where anyone with an internet connection, anywhere in the world, can easily find other business listings.

For example, you can go to Yelp if you are looking for a specific publishing company with positive reviews.

Most customers appreciate the convenience of instantly locating a business online. Businesses can register on these sites, create a profile and promote themselves to a global or regional audience.

- Yelp for business

- Google My Business

- Bing Places for Business

· Better Business Bureau

· LinkedIn

· Facebook Messenger

· Whitepages

· Yellow book

· Yext/Mapquest

· Citysearch

· Local.com

· Angie's list

· US Directory

· Foursquare

· TomTom

· Manta

· InfoUSA

· EZlocal.com

· Bizjournal.com

· YP.com

Other Free or Low-cost Online Classified Advertising Sites

Like magazine and newspaper classifieds, online classifieds can help your business to reach new audiences.

Craigslist,

ClassifiedAds.com

Geebo

The above three online sites offer free classified advertising compared to social media advertising which can be beneficial but costs money.

Although online advertising sites are unconventional, more people are spending time on the internet, and have made them a more reliable form of advertising.

For example, an Activewear company paid for an online advertising site to direct traffic to its business website. Aside from the increased purchases, they could interact with a more engaged audience.

Also, customers love to check out local listings to see what businesses around them,are offering.

By strategically placing your ads using targeted postal zip codes, cities, states, or countries, you can reach your clients and persuade them to buy from

you.

Grand Opening Coming Soon

Chapter Six

Holidays Sales & Grand Openings

Grand Opening Events

THESE EVENTS ARE BIG occasions for many businesses and a chance for free publicity from the media and to draw crowds into their places of business. Some retail stores could have a two-day grand opening sale.

Grand Openings are great for new businesses. Promote your grand openings by distributing flyers door-to-door, sending postcards, and emails. You could offer free food, ice cream, discount coupons or gifts for the first 10, 20, or 50 customers, depending on your budget. Set a time for a grand opening event, such as the first 2 hours or more.

Provide light entertainment such as live music or disc jockey for an hour or so

Holding a social event to introduce your business to a community can help increase awareness and build relationships. A party with refreshments and special offers on your products and services can make people happy.

For example, when a new business opened its physical shop, it had a grand opening where influencers could try out new releases. Customers were welcome to interact with their favorite influencers and shop at discount prices. As expected, the sales were incredible. The brand received free advertising from customers happy to be associated with the brand.

Grand openings are a great way to build lasting customer relationships.

It is a good idea to place advertisements in online and offline channels for two days; such as the day before the grand opening and the grand opening day.

For grand openings, some companies send invitations to prospective clients or community leaders two weeks before the actual date. To draw large crowds, several retail stores, food establishments, and service businesses could hire professional clowns to walk up and down their businesses' entrances and give out balloons.

Others could have balloons tied around the doors of their business locations. Such activity creates attention.

A grand opening for a new hospital, private clinic, or service agency might benefit the local community. You could invite the mayor of the city and local celebrities. Also, new hotels, car dealerships, or the Introduction of a new product by a corporation might warrant such an occasion.

An example: An ice cream retail chain on the East Coast opened a new store near a college campus.

The grand opening occurred in the middle of February, and after a heavy snowstorm, on a Saturday from 12 noon to 4 pm.

The management and staff of the store received more publicity than they anticipated, and they made the news that day.

They were on the six o'clock evening news, on some local TV stations, radio, and in newspapers. How did they do it? In the first place, opening an ice cream shop in the winter was very intriguing.

Secondly, one week before their opening, they put signs on their display windows announcing the grand opening and FREE ice cream from 2 to 4 pm.

They handed out flyers to passers-by, and the news spread around the city. On the day of the grand opening, two hours before the doors opened, two lines, about half a mile long, formed outside the store.

Adults, students, parents, and children played with snowballs while waiting in line for a free cup of ice cream (from a selection of many flavors).

Surprisingly, the store remained busy with customers several hours after the grand opening. The business has stayed busy since its first day, and is a source of inspiration to many people.

Referrals

Referrals, such as word of mouth, help increase sales for many businesses. Sources of referrals include satisfied customers, other companies, neighbors, nearby businesses, fellow members of organizations, church members, league members, suppliers, vendors, service agencies, associates, family members, and friends.

You can promote referrals by letting as many people as possible know about you and your business and by giving several of your business cards to your contacts.

When your client's interest and excitement in your products or services reflect in their daily dialogues, it creates excitement in the people around them.

Some marketers believe that word-of-mouth advertising is the most effective form of marketing. It is one of the reasons why influencer marketing is quite popular today.

It is nice to connect with your customers instead of collecting new ones who will probably not be frequent buyers. When a business engages, equips, and empowers its existing customers, they are more likely to rave about it to other people who might be interested in your products or services.

As an additional benefit, word-of-mouth advertising is less expensive than other forms of advertising.

Holiday Promotions

Big Holiday Sales Events are common in various parts of the world.

Businesses usually plan, prepare, and participate in special sale occasions such as Father's Day, Mother's Day, Valentine's Day, Independence Day, Thanksgiving, Christmas, and more.

For example, before the popularity of online sales, hundreds of people would stay in long lines outside the entrance doors of large retail stores, several hours before the stores opened, to take advantage of huge discounts on special sale events such as Black Friday.

Some businesses would give huge discounts on high-ticket items. Not wanting to miss the sales, consumers would respond by showing up very early.

Even the people who missed the sale were given rainchecks. Many people would prepay their orders, for future delivery to their homes.

With the advent of online sales, consumers can quickly go online and instantly place an order for free delivery or make other shipping arrangements without having to drive to a store, look for parking space or stay in long lines, to make the purchase.

Many retailers do much of their business on special holidays than at any other time of the year. Holiday sales have proven to be very profitable for these businesses.

What is your target market? Does it consist of working women, men, newlyweds, homeowners, business owners, teenagers, senior citizens, college students, and executives? Send them mailings for special occasions using flyers, discount coupons, direct mail letters, or announcements of special sales events through advertisements in newspapers, radio, television or online.

As part of holiday promotions, some service businesses and several offices have wine and cheese parties for their employees and customers.

Consider this an excellent time to give out business cards and ask for referrals. For example, a service business celebrated its third annual customer week (in early spring) and invited its customers and friends. It was successful in creating customer loyalty and bringing in some new customers.

Press Release

A news release, or press release, is a message sent out to print media, online media, social networks, and journalists to announce the launch of a new product or service.

Types of press releases:

*Product Press Releases containing descriptions of a product and images,

*Event Press Release containing the date, time, location, and description of an upcoming event, *Book Launch about the publication of a new book, *General Launch Release about an upcoming new product or service, and

*Brand press releases to showcase an achievement of a new or existing brand.

Structure

The structure of a press release should include an Eye-Catching Heading, an Introduction, The Body or Description with a photograph or video, and a Call to Action as to how to request additional information or to register and place an order, or a pre-order for an upcoming new product.

Some press release services assist businesses in distributing these press releases. Some of them also help in writing a press release for a fee.

Here are some free press release distribution services:

OnlinePRNews.com,

PRLog.com,

NewswireToday.com

Here are some paid press release distribution services:

eReleases,

EIN Presswire,

PRWeb and

Issuewire.

A press release aims to generate online and offline news coverage, sales leads, and credibility for your product or brand.

Some newspapers or magazines will give you free editorials if your business, product, or service is newsworthy. Your chances of getting free publicity in a newspaper or magazine will increase if you regularly advertise in the publication.

You might consider a news release containing a cover letter to the editor of the newspaper or magazine, introducing yourself, your business, product, or service, and telling the editor how the product or service will benefit the community.

A glossy photograph of the product or place of business and a description of your product/service will accompany the News Release. If you are lucky to obtain a news release with a large news outlet, this will give you additional publicity.

Other Marketing Concepts

Most small, medium and large businesses face a tough challenge now and in the future. This challenge is how to increase sales in the face of rising inflation, increasing competition, a fluctuating economy, relatively high-interest rates, and tight credit.

A marketing concept approach is a foundation for market success. This concept covers three premises:

(1) Need Satisfaction: A business must define its market mission. Specifically, what needs do you want to satisfy? What are the products/services at your disposal to meet these needs? Identify the demographic characteristics of your customers (age, sex, income level, ethnicity, education). What image do you want to project (high price, high quality, low price, excellent customer service, relaxed atmosphere)?

(2) Integration of Marketing Activities:

To increase the probability of capturing a significant market share, adhere to the following factors:

(a) Develop a pricing policy compatible with both the income level of your potential customers and your profit motive.

The profit motive is the desire for individuals and businesses to profit from producing their goods and services.

When businesses are profitable, they can pay wages to their employees, encourage innovation, and set a budget for advertising and other sales promotional activities.

(b) The quality of your products/services should justify your pricing policy.

(c) Create a distribution channel to make your products/services readily and easily available to your potential customers.

(d) Design your promotional strategy to support your pricing, distribution, and marketing policies. Your marketing mixes (product/ service, promotion, price, place of business, and distribution channels) should work together to achieve positive results.

(3) Profit Motive:

While satisfying a need via the proper integration of marketing activities, a company should expect to be profitable. Profitability sustains growth and stability.

(4) Sales promotion should be an ongoing process for all new and established businesses to compete more effectively and capture a more significant market share.

A sales promotional medium should have the following goals to be effective:

(a) Capture Attention: The medium should be such that it will capture and sustain the attention of the potential customer.

(b) Generate Interest: The prospect should find the promotional campaign interesting.

(c) Initiate Desire: The prospect's interest should be strong enough to make them strongly desire the item.

(d) Action: The prospective customer should be motivated to take action by purchasing the product/service.

OTHER UNIQUE WAYS TO OBTAIN SALES

Other Ideas that can contribute to the success of your business:

1. Positive Attitude: The success of a business venture depends on a positive mental attitude and the resources available. A positive attitude requires certain qualities, such as self-confidence, optimism, determination, and perseverance.

An entrepreneur or business manager should refrain from being negative in order to succeed. Get up and use your energies for something positive and creative. If you think negatively, your actions could culminate in failure. Developing a positive thinking habit, equips people with great ideas.

2. Neat, Professional Appearance: Develop a sense and feeling of being professional. A neat and professional appearance enhances credibility and makes customers feel comfortable.

3. Ability to Communicate Effectively: Communication in every organization enhances a successful operation. Good communications require that a message or idea be understood and interpreted as the sender intends. Means of communication could be oral, written, body language, use of signs, and more.

4. Ability to Delegate Responsibility: To obtain growth and expansion, entrepreneurs and managers must assign tasks and duties to subordinates or assistants. Businesses delegate responsibilities to people who can assist in performing the tasks.

5.Adapt to changes in the Business Environment and be Creative: We live in a dynamic society. People keep changing their ideas, priorities, social interactions, tastes, and values. The fluctuating economy affects inflation, unemployment, cost of living, and monetary and fiscal policies. Also important are the rules and regulations that affect the business environment.

6. Be Creative: Monitor your target market and identify changes in consumer demand. Your ability to adapt to these changes requires time and financial investment.

7. Acquire Specialized Training. Education is an investment in human capital and a learning process. Many people still spend much time reading, learning, doing research, writing, and keeping up-to-date. They can gain the first-hand knowledge and experience needed in the day-to-day operations of a business.

8. Ability to Make Decisions Quickly. It is helpful for an entrepreneur to examine all the facts in a given situation and compare them against possible alternatives. They can then analyze the benefits of each choice. The results should provide a meaningful solution and a very logical decision. Many successful entrepreneurs can make quick decisions by maintaining a calm composure and exploring all the facts or alternatives

Chapter Seven

Targeted Emails & Email Newsletters

B USINESS OWNERS CAN BUILD strong relationships with their prospects through targeted email campaigns.

Sending a personalized, targeted cmail is a great marketing strategy and is different from sending the same generic message to your client list.

Cold Email

Businesses send cold emails to someone with whom they have no business relationship.

Businesses use emails and content marketing to generate inbound leads and to follow up by telephone. These emails are brief, to the point, and with valuable content, hoping the recipients will open and read them. Cold emails could arrive in the user's inbox, spam, or junk folder.

If your headline and content are unique, they might catch the reader's attention. If the reader decides to reply, you can then start a conversation and exchange some business ideas.

For example, a clothing company launched a targeted email campaign to its large customer base.

Each email was personalized, based on the category of clothing the buyers liked. As a result, the company generated an increase in sales by approximately 30%.

Newsletter Marketing & Email Newsletters

An email newsletter is a written message sent online to an email list containing news updates and other information about a product, service, or brand.

Visitors to a website or blog can register to join an email list of subscribers and receive monthly newsletters. The information in these newsletters should be valuable to your audience to maintain their interest.

Most people check their emails daily or regularly on their cell phones, iPods, laptops, and other mobile devices.

It can cost businesses less to market by email to consumers than through social media advertising or direct mail.

Every business can create an email newsletter and convert online visitors to subscribers. Begin by designing your welcome email newsletter. Having your list of email subscribers gives you access to their email addresses and sometimes, their telephone numbers.

Two notable differences between Email subscribers and social media subscribers are that the social media platform can shut down a social media account, and you have less control over your subscribers. With email subscribers, you have control and can decide when you wish to contact them.

Some companies that provide email marketing services and enable businesses to create and send emails and newsletters are:

Constant Contact

Hubspot

Aweber

Mailchimp

Constant Contact is popular and has templates that small businesses can use.

Businesses can schedule the sending of email newsletters for any day or time that is convenient.

Many businesses regularly send email newsletters to their client list to promote their brands and increase sales.

Businesses update their customers by providing relevant and helpful information in their newsletters. It also reminds customers of any special discounts or free deliveries.

To promote their brands and attract new customers, businesses send newsletters.

Email Lists

I would be great if you have an in-house email list. If not, you can search online for email list providers where you can purchase targeted lists such as business-to-business email lists, residential email lists, and email lists by industry, zip code, country, state, and city.

Choose a reliable email marketing platform, and give out incentives for anyone to respond to your offer. Tell visitors where to go, such as your website, and how they can make a purchase.

Chapter Eight

Business Cards, Flyers & Brochures

THOSE LITTLE RECTANGULAR BUSINESS cards can do more than show your name and address. They should contain advertising messages such as brand names, hours of operation, and your type of business or specialty. Business cards should look professional, as they can be excellent sales tools.

Give business cards to customers, business associates, people you do business with, and other nearby companies. Business professionals could use business cards more often.

You can have someone put up your business cards on bulletin boards in supermarkets, grocery stores, churches, laundromats, schools, and more.

The reverse sides could have a calendar to make them more functional.

There are also magnetic business cards that customers can stick on surfaces such as the refrigerator.

Even though business cards are essential, some businesses often do not see it, as a chance to market.

Giving your business cards to people could be the best chance to market yourself or your business to a captive audience. Remember to include your email address, website address, and any QR Code that links directly to your web page and people can scan with their cell phones.

Flyers

Have someone distribute your Flyers in busy locations

Flyers are usually just one sheet of paper printed and folded in half. They get people interested in an event, service, product, or idea. They are sometimes called handbills, leaflets, inserts, or circulars, depending on how you use them.

Distributing flyers around the neighborhood and active areas is a marketing strategy many new businesses use. They should be easy to read, so that target customers do not miss your message.

Promoting a new product or service can be as simple as distributing flyers to people and businesses.

Brochures

A brochure is a piece of written information from a business describing its products or services that you give out to people. It explains what you do and how to get in touch with your business. It can be as simple as a one-page brochure folded into three equal parts or a more detailed one.

A brochure can be included with your sales letter, explaining your company's background, products/services offered, and benefits to the user.

Use Attention-Getting Product Displays

When displaying products online or offline, show the best qualities and how the product looks. A shopper would like to see what it looks like, from the front, the back, its color, and other specifications.

Consumers will be willing to buy a product with a display that clearly describes the product.

Use high-quality images and videos

When displaying your products and services, a high-quality display helps to attract your target clients' attention and improves your online visibility.

Customers are more likely to engage with content that has images. Include clear pictures and videos in your product descriptions. They can help attract any hesitant customers.

Professionally taken photographs and videos can help establish your brand's identity. Whether your brand is funny, corporate, or witty, you can use high-quality images and videos to showcase your products and services.

Chapter Nine

Network & Collaborate with others

C OLLABORATE WITH OTHER BUSINESSES to meet the needs of your customers.

How to Network with other Business Owners or Groups

Networking with other business owners or groups is as important as connecting with your customers. It helps you stay in touch with market trends and keeps you ahead of the competition. It sparks business growth and opens you up to new contacts, new perspectives, and new ideas. There are various ways to network with business owners or groups:

Attend professional conferences relevant to your field of expertise.

Join trade fairs relevant to your business.

Ask for connections from acquaintances, family, and friends.

Be active on social media platforms like Twitter and Facebook and join discussion groups relevant to your business.

Add reviews, a video, and any Links to your Landing page

Your landing page may be attracting traffic, but if this traffic is not translating to many sales, your landing page may need to be revised. A visually exciting landing page with proof of sales and links to helpful information relevant to your business can increase your conversion rate.

Adding reviews to your landing page reassures customers about purchasing from your business. When your landing page has valuable and high-quality content, customers can develop an interest in making a purchase.

Explore Other Business Opportunities

It is essential to explore other business opportunities and grow. To explore these opportunities, you could do the following:

· Focus on your core product or service. What do you bring to your prospects? Your specialization is your strength.

· Map your capabilities to your clients' needs.

· Use marketing tools that work for your personality and serve your customers.

· Implement a plan of action that will keep your goals a priority.

Franchising

Franchising is when an owner of a successful business (the franchisor) signs a contract to license the company's operations to someone else (the franchisee) for a fee.

Franchising can be a possibility for established and profitable companies to duplicate themselves in many locations. If you can build relationships with customers and other businesspeople who might be interested in your brand and want to own something similar, you might consider franchising.

Advantages of a franchise to the franchisee:

— Easy raising of capital for an established franchise

— Minimum risk involved

— Instant recognition of a brand name

— Increased distribution channels

— Emphasis on product quality

— Local and national coverage due to cooperative advertising from the home office

Advantages of a franchise to the franchisor:

— Instant increase in sales

— Capital leverage

— Availability of qualified, dedicated, and aggressive management personnel

— Monthly (or weekly) royalties.

Disadvantages of a franchise to the franchisee:

— Payment of franchise fee and other start-up expenses

— Payment of royalty

— Lack of flexibility in buying own supplies or being innovative

— Occasional pressure to meet sales quotas.

Create Licensing Deals

Some successful companies expand their sales through licensing arrangements.

They do this by granting the rights to their intellectual properties to a third party for a fee while at the same time retaining ownership. Such properties include patents, trademarks, copyright, photographs, drawings, and more.

Consult an attorney and a franchise consultant for more details.

Consignment Sales

Advantages & disadvantages

Consignment selling is when your products ship to a dealer (consignee), but he does not pay you (the consignor) until the consignee sells the goods.

The problem with consignment is that the dealer has no capital invested in the products and is not obliged to promote them aggressively. This situation could improve if you work closely with the dealer to ensure that he allocates visible shelf space for your products.

Sellers, businesses, and individuals can profitably use consignment selling. Imagine, what happens when an individual makes a product such as a hand-crafted item, pottery, glassware, or gift item and retail stores do not want to carry or buy them? What happens if someone publishes a cookbook and bookstores do not like to purchase the books to sell in their stores? What happens when a small manufacturer develops a product, but no retailer or wholesaler is willing to invest capital to stock the product? Consignment selling would be an alternative solution.

Some goods, which sell successfully on consignment include light bulbs, farm produce, poultry, eggs, newspapers, crafts, plants, and flowers.

How to use Consignment to Increase Sales

When a consignor provides goods to a seller (consignee), they expect products to fly off the shelves so that they can get their predetermined sales amount. Most businesses opt for consignment sales to sell to people who understand different markets.

With this model, your business would only be concerned with production and reconciling profits with the cost of goods sold.

Businesses that accept goods on consignment rely on suppliers who can provide high-quality products for them to sell. It is essential to ensure that your consignees are pre-qualified or vetted. The most successful vendors are reliable and have a good reputation.

The use of consignment can drive up sales and attract loyal clients. Both the consignor and consignee can be profitable. This strategy enables a business to sell other products without investing any money in acquiring the products.

Yellow Pages and Directory Listings

Unlike online advertising, advertising in the Yellow Pages allows businesses to place their ads for a whole year. Due to the advent of the internet, social media, search engines, and online shopping, the popularity of yellow pages and directory listings have decreased.

Many Businesses are Listed in the Yellow Pages

Although the number of advertisers in the Yellow Pages and other Telephone Book Directories has significantly reduced, businesses can still take advantage of this fact and tap into a proven client base.

You may be surprised to come across a new edition of the Yellow Pages or other telephone book directories. While most people rely on Google to find business contacts, telephone book directories still have several users who flip through the pages occasionally.

An examination of the Yellow Pages shows that there are many categories of business listings. These are the same categories that potential customers will look at, to locate your business.

Your advertisement should complement an old marketing rule using the Five W (s) and the Big H. (Who, What, When, Where, Why, and How.) The goal is to inform the public who you are, what your product or service is, where your location is, when you are open for business, why people should buy your product/service, and how to buy from you.

Here are some reasons people may purchase from you instead of your competitors: better location, free parking on the premises, your reliability, credibility, track record, good reputation, a more comprehensive selection of products, famous brand names, better quality, better service, or lower price.

Export Sales Promotion

Export sales promotions involve sales presentations to overseas distributors who can help sell your products internationally. Presentations can be done one-on-one or online. You can improve your overall business sales by participating in export sales.

Export sales promotion can make a huge difference in profits. Many countries provide incentives for businesses in other countries to trade with their governments and businesses.

Export promotions are a great way to introduce your products and services to new clients and build a reputation for your business.

Persuasively communicating with your customers through export promotions builds customer relationships.

The government encourages businesses to export. The higher the exports, the better the trade balance with other countries. The Commerce Department, with its district offices nationwide, can provide helpful information and services to prospective exporters. Exporting is a suitable method of distributing your products worldwide. It has enabled many businesses to grow rapidly in the past few years.

It is advisable to promptly respond to export sales leads. Delay gives an edge to your competitors. If unable to provide complete details immediately, a brief telephone call or email is an effective way to let the overseas buyer know of your interest.

Follow-Up Letters

When communicating with overseas businesses, follow up with a second letter if you have not received a response from the initial one.

Inform an inquirer that you learned of the company's interest in your products or services through the source identified in the sales lead.

Your local Commerce Department District Office can provide information on overseas firms. You can also do an online search.

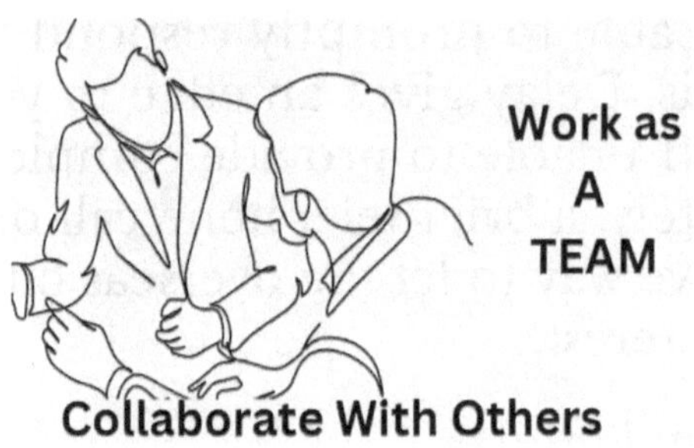
Work as
A
TEAM
Collaborate With Others

Chapter Ten

Direct Mail Marketing

Mail Delivery

DIRECT MAIL MARKETING HELPS many businesses grow by creating brand awareness and generating sales.

To reach their audience successfully, many companies turn to social media marketing and the use of the internet.

The most frequent and widespread use of direct mail marketing is in mailings from businesses to businesses and from companies to consumers by Pizza restaurants, dentists, food delivery services, insurance, retailers, credit card companies, politicians, and others.

For example, a pizza store sent out postcards with an offer of $5 Off, a retail store sent a postcard with an offer of $10 off, and a local fitness center sent a postcard with free admission to the gym for seven days.

Most people show interest by responding to such offers.

In addition to postcards, large companies such as Costco and Sam's Club mail catalogs that display products and discount coupons. Some companies also send sample products to people.

Direct mail marketing continues to be an affordable method of communicating with consumers.

The engagement rate can be high for an offer that provides value and is hard to resist.

Direct Mail Advertising

Many businesses benefit from direct mail advertising with proper targeting and a receptive audience. While email marketing works, direct mail advertising can still be effective.

Direct mail advertising is cheaper than space advertising in magazines and newspapers. Here is how it works: Rent a mailing list or develop your own in-house mailing list. Send everyone on the mailing list your direct mail package mentioned above.

The first and second mailings should be to introduce yourself and provide a summary of your services. Follow-up mailings could be more specific with what benefits these services provide, information on the cost, discounts or gifts you have to offer, any "specials" for the month, and how to place an order.

For example, if an insurance company sends mail addressed to "Current Resident," it is doubtful that anyone goes by that name. The mail could go to the trash unopened, resulting in a very low response.

After a review, the marketing team used modern personalization technology to personalize each mail sent out, and the response rate increased significantly.

Direct mail can be the perfect advertising option if your target clients are progressive people, overwhelmed by digital marketing,

Direct Mail Advertising generates inquiries or sales for a product/service. It serves many objectives, such as offering customers special discounts or notifying them of pre-sale events.

Focus on prospective customers or referrals for new products. Offer specialized products/ services to a selected list of potential customers.

Businesses, professionals, and individuals use direct mail advertising to launch new programs, promote the sale of products/services, announce grand openings, raise funds, generate leads, and promote upcoming events.

Use of Postcards

Businesses use postcards to expand their market or reach: As part of a direct mail marketing campaign, postcards help get your message to consumers inexpensively. You can target specific locations or neighborhoods to create awareness of your product or service.

Postcards can be effective in reaching a specific audience. Some recipients keep postcards for future reference, and some might respond to your offer. The most cost-effective size of a postcard that qualifies for first-class mailing is 4in x 6in size.

Use of Direct Mail Package

It consists of the following: Mailing an introductory letter, along with a brochure, order form, and a return envelope. A faster method includes your website address, email address, telephone number, and a link to where the customer can place an order online.

An objective of the sales letter is to introduce your company and explain the benefits of your product/ service.

An essential part of the direct mail package is that if the recipients are not convinced that you are in a position to satisfy their needs, they may not respond.

The content of the letter should be simple in terms of language. It should be exciting and follow a logical sequence. There should also be an element of informality and a little personalization.

Some reference letters or testimonials from satisfied users would add credibility and create more confidence in what you have to offer. This action can eventually increase your sales.

Suggested ways to promote the value of your product or service are to reduce costs, emphasize the benefits, and offer discount coupons when possible.

Direct mail is successful for selling a product or service that has these qualities:

a) It is a unique product/service.

b) It appeals to many people.

c) The price is affordable.

d) Product is not readily available in neighborhood stores.

e) The quality is good.

Pricing Your Product or Service

Pricing your product or service is essential for success. Your pricing will depend on several variables, such as the price your competitor charges for a similar product/service, your cost of production, distribution, and the price the market can bear. Your pricing will also take into consideration the law of supply and demand.

For example, (a) the price of a product is $25, and you sell ten a month, and suppose (b) the price is $10, and you sell 100 a month. Which is better? $25 X 10 = $250. On the other hand, $10 X 100 equals $1000. The lower price seems better, except if your production or distribution costs are too high to justify a lower price. You could also test other related variables that can help reduce costs.

Chapter Eleven

Radio & Television Advertising

T ELEVISION AND RADIO ADS face much criticism for being expensive, but they can be beneficial for businesses. Often, advertisers run ads to target their radio and television audiences.

TV and Radio enable advertisers to use creative strategies that can resonate with potential customers.

You may want to use TV and Radio advertising to reach the largest segment of your target audience. For smaller audiences, a different promotional strategy may be more effective by narrowing down the demographics.

Radio

Long-distance travelers on highways, workers commuting to work, students, homemakers, and families all listen to the radio at different times during the day. Radio is a source of information, education, and entertainment for many people. Advertisers have used this medium to reach many potential customers. The objective is for your message to be at the right place at the right time.

You can schedule a Radio commercial within a short time. The lower cost of a radio commercial than television makes it an attractive advertising medium. Radio and television stations know who their listeners are, their ages, income levels, and other details through surveys conducted by research agencies. Such information can help the advertiser to locate the radio station that caters to its target market. Radio advertising can help establish an image for a business and make it easier to identify its product or service.

Many radio commercials use 'spots' of approximately 10, 30, or 60 seconds and can run several times a day or for weeks, depending on the advertising budget.

You could use the services of an advertising agency or contact the station's representative for assistance and guidelines in placing the radio commercial.

Rates would depend on the number of commercials contracted for, the different periods (such as prime time), and whether the station broadcasts on AM or FM.

Depending upon where you are, some stations could negotiate "barter" agreements with advertisers by exchanging products for services. Such an arrangement may be possible when the retailer or small business can provide products or services needed by the station.

Television

Efforts to reach prospective buyers on TV start by speaking to one of its representatives. Research your market and examine television programs to determine the best way to advertise to your target market. The representative knows the profiles of listeners for each of the programs and can help identify your target market. Your local television station may be able to produce your commercial, or you can use the services of a production company.

Advertising Budget

A budget is a necessary factor when developing advertising and sales promotional campaigns in each of the different media.

The budget enables you to control your advertising and sales promotional expenditures. When properly managed and planned, this technique can help you survive the seasonal fluctuations of a business.

Another advantage of the advertising budget is to allocate funds for your busy season and increase sales promotions.

Holiday Promotional Advertising

One exception to the advertising budget is for holiday promotions such as Father's Day, Valentine's Day, Mother's Day, Easter, or Christmas.

On these special occasions, businesses generate additional sales and their advertising costs are higher than usual. In addition to online and social media advertising, businesses can advertise on late-night TV or Radio shows that are less expensive than prime time.

Chapter Twelve

Telephone & Sales Reps

Selling to Individuals by Telephone

SELLING TO INDIVIDUALS IS unlike selling to businesses. A good time to call companies is during working hours, and for households, it would be from about 5 pm to 7 pm when most heads of household are home, getting ready for dinner.

Many businesses sell their products and services using telephone sales representatives. Some telephone sales operations are successfully creating leads, obtaining subscriptions to magazines, making appointments for demonstrations, and following up with marketing campaigns. Some retailers use them to inform their credit card holders and regular customers of upcoming sales.

Advantages of Telephone Sales

Sales representatives find telephone marketing advantageous. Making several phone calls to a pre-qualified list of people to explain the benefits of your product or service can generate some sales, which is cheaper and faster than knocking on doors.

Many telephone sales operations have a supervisor who instructs the salespersons on the proper telephone selling techniques.

Disadvantages of Telephone Sales

With the internet and social media being at the forefront of sales and marketing, telephone sales calls are not as popular as they were in the 1980s. Also, many people and businesses do not trust unknown callers trying to sell something and prefer receiving the information by email, direct mail, or online.

A telephone sales operation with a dozen or more sales reps would continuously motivate its employees to achieve their goals.

Selling to Businesses by Telephone

You could try to obtain a list of other businesses from your local Chamber of Commerce when selling to businesses. A good time to reach many business owners is between 10 am and 12 noon and from 3 pm to 5:30 pm.

The decision maker you want to contact in a business could be the Office Manager, the Vice President, President, or the Buyer.

There are several objectives of telephone sales. The most common are product sales, lead generation, or invoice payments.

Businesses can give incentives such as; free lessons for a limited time, offered by some learning institutions, health spas, weight loss clinics, or clubs.

Selling by Invoicing Net 30 days

An invoice is a written statement of the products or services a consumer purchases, the amount due, and how to make a payment.

Businesses usually send invoices to other companies and consumers, payable in 30 days or as agreed upon by both parties.

Businesses can deliver a paper invoice by hand, postal mail, email, or fax.

Other ways of actively using the telephone to generate income include the following:

a/: Sales Leads. Various small businesses, such as repair services, cleaning services, and fundraising groups, use the services of telephone sales representatives to generate leads.

b/: Market Research and Surveys: Several organizations, research firms, and institutions occasionally conduct surveys and polls by telephone.

c/: Answering Service: Some independent home workers and businesses use telephones as answering services for other companies.

d/: Bill Collection: Many bill collectors for businesses and financial institutions use telephones to call up debtors to remind them of their past due bills and arrange possible repayment plans.

Chapter Thirteen

Newspapers & Print Advertising

RETAILERS, FOOD ESTABLISHMENTS, AND service businesses consider newspaper advertising a primary and necessary medium. Your product/service receives local coverage. The increase in your sales volume indicates the result of your advertising.

A business-related product or service should have its ad tested in a business publication or a trade magazine. Your local newspaper and publications would be your best bet to try display and classified advertising.

For example, my research indicates that the best months for book sales through advertisements in newspapers/magazines and mail orders in general are January, February, March, Apr il, September, October, and November.

Therefore, we should minimize such advertisements in the summer months. Newspaper ads are very effective on Sundays and usually cost more than on other days because more people read the papers on Sundays than on any other day.

Classified advertising

The most economical method of newspaper advertising is classified advertising. For a business promoting itself on a shoestring, classified advertising is a good buy because of the high exposure obtained relative to cost.

Many publications could help compose your ad at no extra charge. New businesses, as well as many established businesses, use classified ads weekly or regularly. Many of these publications are also online.

Additionally, classified advertising is an easy way to build an in-house list of potential customers. A method of doing this is to offer to send out a free brochure for more information about a product or service.

Our survey of classified sections of some national and local newspapers shows that action words and descriptive words are used to start the classified ads. They effectively create attention, make readers notice your ad, and make it stand out. Such action and descriptive words include:

"Order Now, Save; Free; Sell; Increase; New& Improved; Act Now, Fabulous, Amazing, Lovely, Stand," and many more.

Display advertising is another method of advertisement in a newspaper or magazine, which are also online.

If your display ad ends with a discount coupon, it serves two important purposes. It tends to increase the response rate as more people like to make purchases at the best possible price, especially on discounts.

You can also measure your response rate this way. As customers send back the coupons, you can determine the number of responses to your display ad. Many food establishments, health clubs, and several service businesses have used this method successfully with coupons for "two for the price of one," "half-price sales," and other discount rates.

Great Product/Service
Price
Place
Promotion
Channels of Distribution

Chapter Fourteen

Bid Lists & Government Contracts

GOVERNMENT CONTRACTS ARE A cost-effective way to grow your business revenue. Governmental agencies often sign contracts to buy products or services from small businesses.

There is no guarantee that every business can win a government contract because it is very competitive. However, you can take some steps to:

• Identify the type of product or service that governmental agencies would need.

• Start with small contracts, establish a few wins, and build a track record of delivery. It is an indicator that you can deliver on the big contracts.

• Focus on a few areas to build credibility with governmental agencies.

• Offer competitive pricing and high-quality products and services.

• Review your completed bid before submitting it to ensure you have all the required documents. Most government agencies are strict when it comes to paperwork.

Contracts From Other Businesses

Corporate purchasing offices accept competitive bids for various products and services. Suppose you have a product or service to sell to X.Y.Z. Corporation. You could send them an introductory letter, telephone the person in charge of purchasing, or make an appointment to introduce yourself in person. A practical approach would be a combination of all three.

During the initial consultation, you could request to be placed on their bid list for upcoming projects that may require your service or product. You could follow up with monthly or bi-monthly mailings.

The idea is to keep your product or service in the minds of the purchasing agents of X.Y.Z. Corporation so that when the need arises, you could be considered.

Contracts from the Government

The government buys a wide variety of goods and services from businesses.

Information on government buying methods, specifications, and advice are provided to businesses through the offices of the Small Business Administration.

The government buys practically every category of most goods and services, from food products, medicines, airplanes, ships, paper, ink, computers, clothing, books, tissue papers, photographic equipment, office machines, and equipment to consultant services, construction work, medical, legal, accounting, and other services.

One of the ways to find contracts is to get on bid lists by registering with a government agency. Most bid proposals can be reviewed, completed, and submitted online, with follow-up by email or telephone.

XYZ PRODUCTION CO.
THE BEST IN TOWN
CALL 421-0000

Chapter Fifteen

Indoor & Outdoor Advertising Signs

Rentable Billboards

ON THE SIDES OF some major roads, you can find billboards covered with different advertisements for different products and services. Billboards can be effective in attracting customers due to their eye-catching displays. Billboards and signs are on highways and in high-traffic outdoor locations.

While some ads run for a few hours daily, others are displayed until it is time to replace them. This continuous exposure ensures that passers-by are reminded of your business whenever they catch a glimpse of your billboard.

Businesses have the choice of where they would like to place their ads based on the behavior of their target market. By choosing the right location, a company can reach all the right people and encourage them to visit its website or physical store.

Advertisements on billboards allow potential clients to learn more about your business.

Other Signs

There are many other types of signs, such as Advertising Signs, Display & Sidewalk Signs, Outdoor Signs, Window signs, and Storefront Signs.

Advertising signs can be inexpensive, and display valuable information about a business. Some storefront signs have lights that make them visible, both day and night. They create brand awareness which can convert to sales.

A business can use signs for functional purposes such as directing potential clients to a store or branding. Some signs display the logo of the company.

Sidewalk Signs

Some retail businesses such as restaurants, use sidewalk signs to promote their daily specials. On a busy street, sidewalk signs can attract walk-in traffic to businesses.

They can attract impulse buyers and are afford-able advertising alternatives, especially for new businesses.

Think about the times you have walked into a restaurant because its sidewalk sign showed the daily specials coupled with the sensational smell of food. As always, businesses enjoy loyal customers when they provide quality products and services.

Indoor Bulletin Boards

You can use indoor bulletin boards to dis-play any message. Using indoor bulletin boards can be profitable if the message is short, easy to read, and understandable. A visual concept placed in a common area can get attention in ways emails and ads cannot.

For instance, a coffee shop uses a bulletin board to advertise its house coffee blend. Every time customers walk in, they can see the bulletin board right before they pay for their order, and can result in sales. Regular customers may want to occasionally try the house coffee blend and gives them a chance to sample it.

Many supermarkets, apartment complexes, schools, colleges, churches, large office buildings, recreation halls, and community centers have bulletin boards for individuals, organizations, or businesses.

Window Signs

Window Sign

Many retail businesses use Window and Door Signs to let customers know their hours of operation. In retail merchandising, advertising begins with appearance and how well the window signs show.

In busy locations, window displays could be of unique value to the retailer and a source of valuable sales promotion.

Many outdoor signs on business locations display the business name and logo and help to find or locate the business quickly.

Some other signs are portable, changeable copy signs, OPEN and CLOSED signs, and SPECIAL SALE signs.

SIDE WALK SALE

Chapter Sixteen

68 Ways to Obtain Customers

O BTAINING AND MANAGING NEW accounts is a great way to build customer relationships, plan business continuity, and discover growth opportunities.

Customers help businesses stay up and running. Your business can be profitable for years if the flow of customers is steady.

When creating a marketing campaign, think about your potential clients. Understand how they would choose between two similar products and use strategies that would trigger a positive reaction.

Attracting new customers based on their preferences helps a business to grow.

Here are 68 ways businesses can attract new customers and retain existing ones:

1. Delay is not a refusal to buy

Some consumers may delay purchasing high-ticket items for various reasons, such as needing more time, additional information, or resources to make the purchase.

Finding a solution to the needs of such consumers can help increase sales, customer satisfaction, and retention.

2. Increase your customer base

When you provide free valuable content in your messages, consumers are more likely to share your information and increase your customer base. Your content and messages could also go viral and turn an unknown entity into a household name.

Companies that provide interesting and valuable content in both print and online engagement with their audience on social media networks, and ask for referrals, can increase their customer base.

Online businesses can host webinars or post videos to share with their audience and make them remember your brands when purchasing.

3. Create demand for product or service

You can create excitement for your brand by emphasizing the benefits it provides to the consumer, such as the added value it brings to the customer, its limited availability, and creating a sense of urgency to buy.This strategy can increase the demand and sales of your product or service.

Businesses need to understand their buyers and what motivates them. They can then translate their needs into solutions, by providing benefits of their products or services.

Businesses can accomplish this through ongoing communications, consumer engagements on your website, online forums, webinars, live presentations, and advertising campaigns.

Businesses can monitor the results of promotions by using analytical tools to measure traffic and manage content.

4. Use Webinars, Podcasts, and Online Presentations

Businesses can reach many customers simultaneously through Webinars and Online Presentations. They are a great way to connect and interact with customers.

Businesses can enable their audience to remember their brands by hosting webinars, podcasts, or posting videos.

Tell your customers why they need to join your webinar or online presentation. Many webinars and online presentations are live, but some are pre-recorded events that can help generate leads and potential sales.

Organize the webinar or online presentation around a problem and offer a solution to this problem. Use a topic that is irresistible to their target audience. · Provide information that unites your target audience and draws their attention.

5.·Be proactive.

Identify and resolve little problems before they turn into bigger problems. Take steps to maintain a positive business environment, and be approachable, polite, and friendly in your interactions with your audience.

Your customers or clients will appreciate you when you display self-confidence, a sense of urgency, a healthy and lifestyle.

For example, many restaurants were not open during the COVID-19 pandemic in 2020. Restaurants and other businesses globally could have lost hope and completely shut down. Instead, they chose to remain positive by devising new methods to serve their customers, such as home deliveries and curbside pickup.

6. Recruit affiliates through online promotions

Using independent marketers to refer your products and services to their audiences is one way to broaden your reach. Recruit new affiliates by announcing and promoting your affiliate program online and offline.

The more affiliates you recruit, the more sales you are likely to make. As such, it is in your business's best interest to give them incentives by offering tier-based performance rewards. Affiliates usually have affiliate links that they share with their network.

7. Use Qualifying phrases

Businesses use adjectives such as; new, improved, incredible, unique, fantastic, wonderful, beautiful, fun, scary, strange, helpful, and ridiculous in promotional materials. These words can add impact to your advertising messages and create more sales.

8. Provide High-Quality Product/Service

Introduce new or better-quality products. More and more consumers are well-educated and have adequate disposable incomes. Most consumers would often prefer a better-quality product at a higher price than a low-quality one.

Find ways to improve, such as faster service, better products, a more attractive package, or longer business hours.

9. Meet the Needs of Customers

You will first need to research your customers before launching a product or service through advertisements.

Conducting surveys makes it easy for businesses to ask questions about specific things they would like to know. They can then summarize their findings to determine what their customers have in common.

10. Start with your past and present customers

Developing an existing account is less expensive than obtaining a new one. Re-examine your customers' needs to find out if there is a new trend. Changing lifestyles could affect the demand for a product/service. Keep satisfying their needs in terms of good products, excellent service, and, occasionally, new product introductions.

11. Ask for referrals

Sales referrals mean that people familiar with your product or service are willing to tell their families, friends, co-workers, and other businesses about you.

Offer your present customers a discount or an incentive for every referral they bring. Special sales, deals, and incentives, combined with publicity and advertising, always get the attention of new and existing customers.

Customers can also give you the contact information of those interested in your brand. You can then follow up by contacting such leads.

Businesses can also ask customers or clients for referrals when sending them invoices.

Other ways to ask for referrals could be by telephone, in person, email, websites, and online forums.

Always be polite, friendly, and courteous when asking for a referral.

How to Ask for Referrals from Customers

A referral customer is cheaper to acquire than other non-referred clients, and they have a higher potential to remain loyal. Be active in your networks without seeming desperate or making the interaction awkward.

Here are a few ways for businesses to ask for referrals from customers:

• Send referral emails that mention your work with the recipient. It gives incentives and has a call to action on how they can proceed to refer your business.

• Be specific with your referral request; chances are, your customer will not mind referring your business to family, friends, and acquaintances if they are satisfied with your product or service.

• Focus on your most active customer relationships because your customers are more likely to give positive feedback.

Customer referral builds goodwill and brings clients who need your products or services to your business.

Build relationships and interact with your customers to obtain as many referrals as possible.

12. Develop a direct-sales staff or representatives

Developing a sales staff is a successful selling strategy.

For example, an entrepreneur invented and manufactured an electric wheelchair. Sales were slow until the company recruited several satisfied customers as sales representatives, who were actual users, and sales increased.

Some door-to-door salesmen give out free balloons with their names and advertising messages imprinted on them to children in homes they visit. While they are busy giving sales presentations to parents, the children are busy playing.

13. Promote your content in online and community events

Participation in both online and offline events increases brand awareness and the visibility of a business. Social contacts that could result in increased prospects include meetings of various associations, online forums, business meetings, seminars, trade shows, other social events, and speaking engagements.

14. Follow up on leads/referrals and cold calls

Businesses should plan to follow up on all leads by phone, email, text message, or in person.

The more calls one makes, the better the chances of getting a new account, especially from users of competitive products who might not be satisfied with their current vendors.

The worst that could happen if one tries and fails is to be right back to where one started.

15. Word-of-Mouth Marketing

Word-of-mouth sales are when you exceed your customer's expectations, and they are happy and willing to tell others about your business.

Off-line, satisfied customers will tell their co-workers and people they know about the great experience they had at your company.

They can post their positive experience online on blogs and other online forums.

Other bloggers can easily repost to generate free advertising and publicity for your business. Small businesses have become successful through word-of-mouth advertising. It is an effective as well as the least expensive form of advertising.

For example, some time ago, a successful business started as a single retail store. The business grew to hundreds of stores in the United States and overseas. The company has high customer loyalty and retention rates, word-of-mouth referrals, and provides excellent customer service to online and offline customers.

As of 2022, they are still very successful, both offline and online, where they have a strong presence. The company has built customer loyalty and retention by providing excellent customer.

16. Ask for Recommendations from Satisfied Customers

Aside from the people who engage in production or your employees, no one knows your product better than a repeat customer. They can recommend your brand to everyone they know. Individuals representing your company's brand to their audience are brand ambassadors.

When a company offers incentives to such people, they may be willing to go out and help raise awareness of your brand. They can do so because they know your brand and what it stands for. Others, such as affiliate marketers, usually receive commissions from the company for sales. Affiliates typically have affiliate links that they share with their network.

17. Free trials can generate sales

Companies offer free trials to generate sales for products such as computer software, apps, games, and many more. Free trials generate sales for the company and produce customer satisfaction.

Many companies offer limited-time free trials, and consumers are happy to test-drive a product or service before making the purchase.

18. Join Social Media Groups such as Chat Groups. Book Clubs, Business Groups, and others

Groups are an excellent way for people with similar interests to get together and discuss them. Your group can be about a topic or writing and include friends and people you don't know. The main goal is to get people to discuss.

You can join existing online groups in your area of expertise or form a new one.

To start a group, you'll need to find people to join. You can do this by telling people about your group or by putting up flyers or online ads.

Set up a good time and place for everyone who wants to be there. The key to a successful group is to have valuable conversations.

19. Stay Positive by Showing Confidence & Persistence

Staying positive and persistent are essential tools in life and business. Often, companies will go through trying times when sales are not what was projected or expected, and it can be hard to stay positive during these periods.

Take steps to maintain a positive business environment by looking and acting professionally, being approachable, polite, friendly, and proactive by interacting with your audience.

Business owners and managers should be open to questions and answers, possess self-confidence and a sense of urgency, and have a healthy and active lifestyle.

20. Valuable Content and transparency

Provide content that informs potential customers of what your business does. Seek your customers' opinions and use the information collected to improve customer experience and measure customer satisfaction.

By providing valuable content to your customers, you can increase the value of your business, customer retention, and customer base. It is necessary to ensure that you have as many loyal customers as possible.

You can maintain excellent customer support and service by acknowledging and listening to customers' needs.

Customers can also obtain accurate and up-to-date information about your business from online search engines.

When your business consistently provides value, it becomes easy to increase your client base.

The goal is for consumers to remember your business, come to you for solutions, become a client or customers, and increase your customer base.

21. Offer a variety of products and services

Offer variations of your products or related and similar items so that customers can choose what to buy, such as various sizes or price points.

For example, a book publisher can have variations of the same book in a printed book, eBook, softcover, hardcover, or audio versions.

Other examples are televisions that come in different sizes and technological levels, such as intelligent televisions.

Some service providers have various specialties and offer related services in addition to their regular services.

Vehicles come in various models and engine types, such as gasoline-powered, hybrid, diesel, or electric.

22. Search Engine Optimization (SEO)

SEO is how we optimize our content on search engines by using keywords. The goal of using SEO is to help increase website ranking and traffic to your website or blog and create brand awareness that can result in sales.

23. Use of Mystery Shoppers to increase the quality of service

These are secret shoppers a company pays to shop in its stores as well as in a competitor's.

The secret shoppers report back to the company on several things, such as the quality of products and services, the attitude of employees or sales associates, the response time to acknowledge a customer, the wait times at checkout, and other information needed about your competitor or your business.

The company then uses this information to improve customer service and attract new customers.

The use of mystery shoppers helps to improve customer service and provide a better shopping experience and hopefully make your business more appealing than that of your competitors.

It is necessary to conduct competitive analysis, and many small and large businesses do so.

It is incredible how owners of businesses were unaware of some mistakes and errors in their operations until discovery. These businesses then take corrective actions to improve the customer experience and potential sales.

24. Show customer appreciation

Show customers that you are grateful for their business. Thank them for being valued customers. This gesture creates customer loyalty, possible repeat sales, and long-term business relationships.

25. Reference Selling

It is known as reference selling when happy customers or clients are willing to voluntarily tell others about your business, product, or service. Positive testimonials or references help to build trust, reliability, and credibility for your product or service.

Remember to obtain permission from these customers before using them as references. Obtain their names and telephone numbers and, if possible, provide some incentives.

Encouraging customers to provide reviews and positive feedback is a great way to bring in new customers and build customer loyalty.

26. Respond to Sales Objections

Consumers sometimes object to purchasing for several reasons, including price, quality, durability, need for additional information, a demonstration of the product, and more.

Businesses can respond to objections by listening, asking questions, emphasizing the product or service's benefits, offering special incentives or discounts, and following up with the customer. Ask for the sale after addressing all questions and concerns.

27. Collaborate and Network with Others to Increase Sales

Some valuable ways to collaborate with other businesses include Sharing office or retail space, sharing paid advertising costs, and referring your customers to other companies with different specializations. They will reciprocate by referring their customers to you, participating in joint projects or ventures, forming a business merger agreement with a smaller competitor, joining a team, and sharing documents and other important information.

28. Create Impulse Sales

Impulse buying is when customers purchase products or services they are not planning to buy. Some typical impulse buys are snacks such as candy, food, groceries, clothing, shoes, and other items when they are displayed near the checkout register or at discount prices. Consumers frequently buy impulse items while shopping.

29. **Suggest add-Ons at checkout.**

Suggesting add-ons at checkout is an indirect sales technique called suggestive selling. The idea is to recommend at least one additional product or service you think might benefit the customer, such as an extended warranty. If the customer makes the extra purchase, they will thank you for making the suggestions and, more likely, will convert to a repeat customer.

Remember to treat your customers like friends and ask them for suggestions about what product or service they would like you to offer.

For example, when you purchase a dinnerware set online, you can get add-ons such as gift wrapping, a card, a tip, and product replacement insurance plans. During the holiday seasons, gift-wrapping add-ons are popular additions to sales. This strategy is effective because customers can get a better experience, especially if a business offers something that is an excellent addition to their purchase.

30. **Influencers**

People with influence over a large audience can generate good content about your brand for their audience. They can keep the viewers engaged, comment on your product or service, and possibly develop new sales. Collaborating with influencers can be very effective and allows them to promote your brand to their audience.

Influencer marketing can be cost-effective during the holiday season, build credibility, be targeted, and save time.

31. Mention your business in meetings and social gatherings

When you meet new people in meetings, introduce yourself and hand out business cards. Mingle or move around during breaks, smile, and greet others.

Listen to other people and engage in discussions. Stay calm and not appear too anxious to meet new people, knowing they might be your potential clients or customers.

32. Attend trade shows, fairs & events

You get a chance to meet face-to-face with potential clients/customers at trade shows. Talk about your business, receive instant feedback and hand out your promotional materials.

Participate in trade shows, fairs, and special events to show your presence and let potential customers see the strengths of your product or service. Businesses can use this opportunity to interact with other companies and expand their market.

33. Give away gifts and promotional items

When shoppers receive a gift or an extra incentive, they are more motivated to spend more money at your place of business. Consumers will also be more inclined to tell others about their positive experiences.

Suggested places to give out free samples or gifts could include areas where potential customers go, such as shopping malls, trade shows, fairs, and special events, online on your website and blogs.

34. Ask for Reviews from Satisfied Customers

Reviews and positive consumer feedback give credibility to your brand and build trust. For example, a business with hundreds of 5-star reviews will attract more customers than a similar business with 3 –star reviews. Positive feedback helps businesses generate new sales leads and retain existing customers.

35. Present a Neat & professional Appearance, work environment, or location

Businesses that offer a neat and professional work environment create a positive atmosphere that attracts people who want to do business with you. Your online store, website, or blog should also look professional.

36. Share your Successes with Customers

You can compile and present case studies on your website, blog, social media, marketing video, webinars, sales presentations, and other sales materials.

Explain how the customer overcame a challenge and how your product or service helped meet and achieve customer satisfaction.

Share these success stories in advertising/marketing campaigns and social media to help bring in new customers.

37. Give out Business Cards, flyers, or brochures more often

They are necessary for promoting your brand. They let people know who you are, your business type, and how they can contact you. They open doors to initial conversations, follow-ups, and future discussions about your product or service.

38. Broadcast your services or products on Websites & Social Media

Publish a webinar, podcast, or blog on social media to educate your potential customers. Consider using a spokesperson (like the celebrities do), a publicist, a representative, or an ambassador to help publicize your business. They can showcase your business at trade shows, live-streaming, and promotional campaigns.

39. Encourage Customers to visit again to generate repeat sales

Use phrases such as "thank you, come back again," "hope to see you soon," and "enclosed is a 10 percent coupon good for your next visit".

It is a great idea to notify your existing customers before launching any new products or services so that they will be one of the early ones to become repeat customers. Repeat customers are loyal to your business and more willing to spend money than one that does not know you.

Offer a discount code if appropriate for your type of business: Several retail and online companies offer promotional codes, coupons, discounts, or vouchers as incentives for repeat customers. These can result in additional sales and bring in new clients.

40. Respond to questions & inquiries on time

Responding to inquiries helps to prevent negative online feedback and can turn bad reviews into positive ones. It shows that the business cares by taking the time to answer questions from consumers. It results in better customer satisfaction.

41. Give to a charitable cause

Companies give to charitable organizations to promote goodwill, corporate image, and brand.

It makes consumers happy when businesses support a favorite cause.

Acts of charitable contributions include giving money, valuable time, or expertise to religious groups, nonprofit organizations, and fundraising events.

42. Create an online event

Before the Covid-19 Pandemic, Sales executives organized and participated in live in-person events such as trade shows, product demonstrations, and others. The costs associated with such events included travel expenses, the cost of the conference room or venue and refreshments, lodging, and accommodation.

During Covid-19, most people worked remotely from the comfort of their homes. Many organizations could reach their customers by switching to virtual events, such as webinars, podcasts, blogs, websites, and live streams.

The challenge was promoting the virtual event by sending out 2 to 3 emails, followed by reminders using text messaging, voice messaging, or telephone calls.

Reminder to record your virtual event so that you can use it as a replay of the event later, or

send to those who could not attend initially due to their busy schedules.

43. Plan a local business workshop

Organizing a workshop or local town hall meeting style allows people to interact with other local business owners, exchange ideas, join together to advertise as a group, and swap email lists. Participants could connect and provide opportunities to generate new business leads.

You can also coordinate a small workshop, either online or in-person, to celebrate an event such as an anniversary, a new month, back to school event, a first-time home buyers event, and many more.

44. Sponsor a local sports team

Sponsoring a local sports team can increase brand awareness and goodwill in the local community. Such sponsorship can benefit the team, the athletes, and the business.

The goal of the business is to reach your potential customers by generating leads and sales. Another benefit is the coverage it receives from radio, television, print, and social media networks.

45. Expand by acquiring other businesses

Companies acquire or merge with other businesses when the right opportunity comes along.

Businesses can increase market share, expand their customer base and reach new markets through acquisitions, mergers, consolidations, asset sales, and more. It makes the companies grow faster and become more competitive.

46. Email Prospecting

Follow up with prospects in several ways, such as: sending them a link to a video of your business or new product. You can also send them a thank you card for taking the time to meet with you, send a birthday card if you know their birthday, or invite several prospects to a complimentary breakfast meeting and offer tea, coffee, muffins, or snacks.

Show a video, and tell your audience about any discount offered if they act now.

When organizing an online event, consider offering a free instant download.

In summary, when using email for prospecting, start by identifying yourself, be brief, offer something of value and finally, thank them for taking the time to read your email.

47. Ask for the order

Reminder to ask for an order and ask customers what else they might need.

48. Use Cold Calling

Cold Calling is when you make telephone calls to strangers hoping to get a sale.

Always start a cold call by stating who you are, where you are calling from, and to whom you are trying to speak. If the person is busy, ask if you can send some information about your business by email.

49. Network and collaborate with other businesses

Remember to follow your planned objective for joining a network or forum, provide helpful advice, content, or something of value/ Introduce yourself, follow up with contacts, ask for advice, and after a reasonable time in the network, introduce them to your product or service.

50. **Verbal & Written Communications can get more sales leads**

Verbal communication takes place through spoken words. It is an essential part of the world of marketing. You can persuade customers by talking to them well

Written communication

Most times, writing does the magic. It entails writing compelling copy with a firm tone that can convince the reader to buy your brand. The overall goal of communication should be clear, concise, and precise.

51. **Add visuals to your Valuable Content**

People are more encouraged to view your online content with visuals, images, or a video. Most people tend to view and process visuals faster than reading text. The old quotation from many years ago that "a picture is worth a thousand words" is still true today, especially on social media, where you see a lot of visuals and images, resulting in better retention

52. **Curiosity Keeps Consumers Engaged**

With technological advances, the internet, online shopping, and instant social media connections, consumers are curious to find more information. Curiosity prompts consumers to request more information, search online or investigate.

Consumers want to know who, what, when, why, and how to decide on a purchase.

53. Follow-up on previous sales

Following up gives you a chance to make sure that customers are happy. It also allows you to answer any questions that might have come up since the last time you talked to them.

54. Target Your Market

Advertise where your target customers are.

Location is important. The right place to market is just as important as the right price if you want to generate some sales.

For online and offline sales promotions, a business that places its products in front of a target audience will generate more sales than a business in a location with no prospects or target customers.

For example, law enforcement and other people who carry guns regularly go to the range to practice how to shoot.

The most important lesson besides gun safety is the ability to aim at your target mark. Many people miss the target either because they do not know how or are not focused.

The goal of this book, "how to promote your business and increase sales," is to enable businesses to stay safe online by protecting their brands and focusing on their target markets.

55. Use Scarcity & Exclusivity

Some businesses use the following words and phrases to create scarcity and increase the demand for their brand: Limited time offer; limited supply; while supplies last; first 50 customers only; 2-day sales; members only; order yours today; online orders only.

This strategy can generate pre-orders or a waiting list of potential buyers.

56. Use Qualifiers in your promotional content

Adjectives like great, lovely, beautiful, fun, scary, strange, helpful, and wonderful can help attract your audience's attention.

They can get people's attention who may want to find out more details about your offer or possibly make a purchase.

57. Offer a limited-time money-back guarantee

A money-back guarantee allows the purchaser of an item an opportunity to return the item within a specified time if they are not happy with it.

Offering such a guarantee can improve business image, improve customer satisfaction and make more consumers want to try a product or service. A money-back guarantee benefits the customer and the retailers.

58. A desire to be competitive and take calculated risks

Such competition could result in a better understanding of your customers and increase market share. You can minimize risks by researching and analyzing a situation before committing.

59. Get Help from Experts

Business owners sometimes struggle with other parts of the business, such as production or marketing. When this happens, employing the services of an expert in a sector you work in can help your business grow to new levels.

Seek help from experts to minimize financial losses and help your business adapt to new markets. Experts have the knowledge you may not have and may not have considered without their help. They bring in a fresh perspective and contribute to your business' growth by ensuring it is profitable.

60: Layaway or buy now, pay later

Many businesses allow customers buying high-ticket items to make a down payment and pay off the balance within 30 days or an agreed-upon time. Upon payment in full, the customer can pick it up from a retail location or make delivery arrangements.

Most consumers using the buy now pay later service are paying cash and do not wish to put their items on high-interest credit cards.

61. Out-of-stock Signs

Many retail and online stores sell out of some items quickly.

A sales strategy is to place an out-of-stock sign next to a color photograph and a description of an item. This action creates inquiries about the item and generates orders while the item is awaiting arrival.

Out-of-Stock signs work well for fast-selling items and the launch of new products.

62. Extended Hours

Inform your customers when you are open for business on special holidays. Holiday shoppers look out for limited-time special holiday sales online and in-store. November and December months are very busy for many companies. At this time of year, most consumers shop not only for themselves but also purchase several gifts for their families and friends.

63. Thank the Customer

Always say Thank You after each sale. It makes the customer feel appreciated, willing to spend more money, and want to return and do more business with you. Thanking your clients or customers shows respect and makes them feel important. It also reinforces in the customer's mind that they have made a wise purchase by patronizing your business.

64. Importance of Asking Questions

By asking customers questions, you can get answers which can lead to sales. Questions such as: How are we doing? Does our product or service meet your expectations? What can we do to serve you better? May we ask for your suggestions on how we can improve our product or service? An easy way to ask these questions is to give the customer a short questionnaire to fill out and return to you. Thank them and provide them with an incentive.

65. Interact with Posts

Interact with posts related to your business line: Create posts or blogs and comment on posts that may interest your customers.

More people become familiar with your business and brand when viewers share and repost your comments.

Your audience can see your post and engage in back-and-forth discussions by adding more comments. Keep your followers or audience engaged by sharing valuable content with them, encouraging them to ask questions, and seeking their advice or opinion.

66. Pre-Launch Sign-ups

Run a pre-launch sign-up promotion before launching your product or service officially.

Always do a pre-launch marketing campaign to create awareness and interest in your upcoming event.

During pre-launch, you can take pre-orders, do a press release to include valuable and helpful content, provide giveaways and announce your launch on social media and offline platforms.

67. Willingness to Adapt to Different Markets

Businesses should be willing to adapt to different markets, such as local, online, mobile users, regional and international markets.

Businesses can fulfill the needs of consumers by providing quality goods and services at affordable prices.

The needs of consumers can be different at various levels. Businesses can learn about consumer needs by acknowledging their social media comments, feedback, reviews, and surveys.

68. Prizes for local fundraisers

Some businesses, known as sponsors, donate prizes to local nonprofit fundraising events, schools, hospitals, religious organizations, and others to increase brand awareness and create goodwill in a community.

Winners can receive prizes such as free pizza, baked goods, gift certificates, gift cards, signed books, sports items, movie tickets, car wash, and more.

Chapter Seventeen

350 Ways to Promote Books/Courses

Social Media Tactics

I T MAKES SENSE FOR businesses to be active on social media because it affects consumer behavior.

Knowing where your audience has the most influence on social media is essential.

Add your social media address to your promotional materials. It lets you reach many of your peers and readers while keeping a professional and easy-to-manage presence. Here are some actions to take:

1. Let People Know about Your Special Projects & Achievements

Let your family, friends, colleagues, and acquaintances know about your special projects and achievements.

2. Post pictures of Your Brand on Social Media

Ask your clients, audience, and fans to take a picture of your product and post it on social media. A better way to get people to share content is to ask them to share things that reflect the experiences and practices of life that your product promotes.

3. Invite users to talk on video

No matter your content, making a video can help connect an audience to your Brand.

You can invite your readers to talk about your book in a video. Businesses can ask customers or clients to talk about their experiences on video.

4. Talk Shows

Many authors speak on Podcasts, Radio, and TV Talk Shows.

Here are some valuable social media platforms:

Linkedin

LinkedIn is popular on social media, and many businesses and professionals use it.

5. Create a Profile

Fill out your profile and inform the audience of your expertise, special projects, honors, and awards.

6. Showcase your Books on Linkedin

In the publications" section, you can list books you have written or helped write, along with a summary and a link to find more information.

7. Connect with Your Audience on LinkedIn

By letting you import your contacts into the system, LinkedIn makes it easy to connect with people you already know. You can then choose to send a LinkedIn connection request to those people.

Platforms such as LinkedIn lets you link your Twitter profile and three other websites to your profile. You can connect your author page, website, and Facebook page.

Some platforms let you connect your social media accounts.

As part of your static profile, Twitter, Facebook, and other social media sites always allow you the chance to link to your homepage.

You can also connect to other sites. Linking to other websites is a common way to get people to notice your site.

8. Join Groups on LinkedIn

There are many business-related topics, and you can join as many groups as you want. Over time, people in the group can figure out what you do when you add valuable content.

Consider joining a Writers' Group. Through these groups, you can talk to other authors to get and give advice, or you can trade books.

9. Create a Group

You might want to start your group on LinkedIn, which is free and can help you get attention.

10. Recommendations

The purpose of LinkedIn's recommendations features is to help users find jobs. You can also ask for recommendations for your business, your book, or yourself as a speaker.

11. Use Endorsements

People can quickly "vote up" your skills and expertise by clicking a button. When you edit your profile, you can add the skills you want people to know you,

12. Useful Content

LinkedIn has a news feed, and people pay attention to it. Many LinkedIn users sign up for daily emails that tell them what people in their networks have been doing.

13. New Connections

Check your LinkedIn invitations at least once a week to accept new requests from people who want to connect with you.

14. Use your Books

Putting your book on LinkedIn is a great way to get people interested. The company would be the publisher's name, and the title would be the name of your book.

15. Good Picture

Find a picture of yourself or take one that looks professional and friendly.

A headshot of your happy, well-groomed face works best.

16. Create Anticipation

Make posts about your work-in-progress in the three to four months before your book comes out.

17. Engage Your Network

Use quotes from your book to create engagement.

By taking small pieces from your book and sharing them with your network, you can get people interested in it and convince them to read the whole book.

18. Share Testimonials

Share a story from a review or a natural-looking and exciting testimonial.

19. Consistency with Posts

Be consistent with your posts, and people will notice and interact.

Google Ads

Most authors who use Google Ads think it is essential that every dollar they spend on advertising works as well as possible. People can type a keyword from the title of your book, and it will appear in search engines.

20. Goals of an Ad on Google

The objective of an ad is to catch your target market's attention and generate some leads.

21. Audience's Questions

Think about their specific questions and wants, and then change the book's content to answer their questions and needs.

22. Target Different Locations

Use the advanced location options during and after your campaign design for the best location targeting.

23. Use Content to Aim

Content targeting, which can involve using keywords, placement, and topics, lets you put ads next to content your current and potential customers are watching.

24. Monitor who Sees your Ads on Google

Use the place where the observation will take place to your advantage. This setting won't change who sees your ads or where they show, but it will let you keep track of how well they are doing.

25. Try Different Types of Campaigns

Using different types of ads can help businesses to analyze and know which ads produce the best results. By focusing on your best promotional campaigns, you can achieve more sales.

26. Keep Track of Sales

Tracking both online and offline conversions can improve the quality of your conversions. By combining Google Analytics and Google Ads, you can also enhance the quality of your insights into sales.

27. Be Available

should give your customers the impression that they can always find you and that you are available. If possible, use the location extension in your campaign for Google Ads.

28. Analyze Your Google Campaigns

Always conduct an analysis of your campaigns, pause the ads that are not productive, and look for other strategies to improve sales. Your analytics can help you make an informed decision.

Twitter for Authors

Twitter has a special place in the lives of authors.

At first glance, it may seem complicated for someone who is used to writing hundreds of thousands of words at a time to put their thoughts into approximately 140 characters, but it is not difficult.

29. Create an Account

Businesses can think about reviews, book or product descriptions, elevator pitches, and other similar short pieces of information and post them on Twitter.

30. Give Value

Most authors, writers, and experts find this tip easy to give because they have been providing valuable advice for years. Twitter lets you share it with more people.

31. Tweet Yor Suggestions Regularly

Your nonfiction book is full of helpful little tips, and your fiction book is full of perfect little sentences. Every day, tweet out one or two suggestions.

32. Network with other people

Many professionals end up talking to anyone who approaches them. Instead, you can be more proactive and write down the names of people you want to meet.

Twitter is a great way to learn from other people, whether they are experts in your field or people who work in the media.

33. Create a List

Prepare a list of people you want to get to know better. The list can include well-known authors, editors at publishing houses, and agents. In other words, these people may know somebody who can be helpful to your business.

34. Share Tips from other Experts

To become an expert in your field:

1. Stay up to date with the latest trends and share information with others.

2. Share tips from other people, articles, and other resources that make you known as an expert in your field.

3. Stay in your area of expertise.

35. Give Away Books

People appreciate promotional products that can be valuable to them.

36. Learn about Other People on Twitter

Twitter is a public place you can learn about other people in your fields. Find out what works for them, and then adapt those ideas to your promotional campaigns.

37. Twitter Bio

In your Twitter bio, add clear and detailed information about your expertise. You can also include the When title of your book and a link to your Website, blog, webinar, or podcast.

38. Host a Tweet Chat on Twitter

A word followed by a pound sign on Twitter is called a hashtag. You can host a Tweet Chat to show off your knowledge. Think of a word or short hashtag you can ask people to use during the hour of your Tweet Chat. Your Tweet chat can be a question-and-answer session about your book, or you can take questions from your followers for an hour at a time that you announce on Twitter.

39. Trends

The trending topics are a good way for Twitter users to pick up on current events and retweet them to others.

40. Book Reviewers

You can also be self-serving by using Twitter to find people who review books in your book's category. There will always be a few famous reviewers that everyone knows.

41. Balance work & personal life

Balancing work life with personal life is a good thing.

The same is true for authors on Twitter. Talk about parts of your natural life that are related to your book. People are most interested in stories about pets, relationships, achievements, business, and personal trips.

42. Use a Few Words

For ads, use just a few words. Write your ad like you would with an outdoor billboard. It is incredible how much your few words can convince people.

43. Use images & Visuals

Twitter is a visual platform, so consider checking your content and images to ensure they are what you want to post.

You can also use custom photography or illustrations to make your content interesting.

44. Call to Action

The bait is your copy and how you look. Your call to action is for your audience to buy your product or request additional information.

45. Timing of Ads on Twitter

Twitter is all about the things that are going on at this moment. Use this to your advantage by making ads that fit in with the time. You can tie your ads to significant events or holidays using event targeting.

Facebook Author Page

Although Facebook is very popular and has many users, many authors still have not made a page for their writing or business. Having an author page on social media can be the first step in gathering and growing a group of fans. Give people you meet at book clubs, conferences, and signings a link to your author page.

46. Personal Facebook Account

You will need an email address, username, and password to register. Go to Facebook to get started, fill out the form, and confirm your email address.

47. Proceed

You will see a link in the top right corner of your page's home screen that says "Create." If you choose the page option, you will go to a new screen where you can make your page.

48. Select Community

When you create a Facebook page for an author, you can choose "community or public figure."

After clicking, give your page a name and select a category. As for the Title, you can think of something unique.

49. Profile Picture

Your profile picture should be neat and look professional.

50. Cover Artwork

You can show a picture that fits your type of writing or a picture of your work on the book's cover.

51. Licensed Photos

Be aware of the copyright rules for the photo you want to use. Personal images or stock photos bought online work best here.

52. Use your page to get more email addresses

Authors need to have a good email list. It gives you even more freedom and power in talking to fans. But it can be hard to set up a way to get people to sign up for your email list. Facebook makes it easy to do so.

53. Provide Updates

Facebook can help in selling books and interacting with your readers. You could Think about telling people what you are doing and how your day is going. When you make things personal, people talk to each other more.

54. Live on Facebook

Facebook Live is another available offer. The organizer can go live on a page via video, and people can join the broadcast and make comments as it goes on.

55. Other Authors

Tell your social media audience when another author writes a new book in your area of expertise. You can help your audience to see your post by tagging them.

56. Engage your Fans

Businesses can build relationships, leading to future help and sales opportunities. Engage your audiences by asking them what they think and responding to their comments. Set up a good commenting system and respond to comments thoughtfully to get people talking.

57. Talk About New Books

You can easily make an announcement and share it with your audience through your social media page. Even better, they can click to tell their friends about the good news.

58. Scannable Message

You can divide the content into sections, making it easy to see which parts are the most important.

59. Coming Soon

Use your cover picture to announce a product or book coming soon. Employ a professional graphic designer that can make the image bold and colorful

Facebook Ads

With Facebook ads, you can reach people worldwide, not just through word of mouth.

60. Setup Facebook Ads

By setting up and running ads on Facebook, more people to a site, get more impressions or even increase the number of people who click on them.

61. Facebook Groups

By joining Facebook Groups, you can reach many people at no additional cost.

62. Retargeting

Retargeting works well when people look at particular product pages but do not buy anything or if they have not bought from you in the last three months. You can even reach out to people who have put items in their shopping carts on your site but made no purchase.

63. Price Reduction

There is a good reason why many businesses do not want to lower their prices. Price cuts can occasionally reduce your profit and change people's opinions of your brand. Price cuts work well when you are trying to sell many items quickly.

64. Persistence

Social media advertising is a skill that takes practice to perfect.

Most businesses can make money with a well-made sales strategy for their online advertising.

65. Scarcity

This advertising tip created a fear of missing out on something. Your response rate can increase when you use scarcity in your ads. Let your audience know when quantities are limited, or you are about to run out of supplies.

66. Custom Audience

With Custom Audiences, you can target different groups of users.

Learn how to use Custom Audiences to expand your market share.

67. Website Traffic

To generate traffic to your website, place your web address on business cards, print books, handouts, flyers, bookmarks, postcards, and more.

68. Other Custom Targets

Target people who have used your product or service and collect their telephone numbers or email addresses for follow-up marketing.

69. Behavior of Users

You can target or reach users based on their buying habits, their intentions, how they use their devices, and more.

70. Interesting Headline

Many people will only look at your ad's headline and not read the rest of the content. A great headline can significantly affect your click-through and conversion rates.

71. Use Questions to Generate interest

You can start your ad copy with questions your potential readers might have asked and show how you provided helpful answers.

72. Expertise

When you advertise in an industry with much competition, your potential customers might also see your competitors' ads. You can show people why you are one of the best.

73. Seasonal Ads

Some people think of Christmas, Black Friday, and other holiday ads when they think of seasonal campaigns. You can create your ads on these special days.

74. Audience Segmentation

A platform's insights tool can help you figure out how big and who your audience is. It lets you know how old, male, or female your audience is, as well as their top country and city.

Instagram Promotions

Suppose you want to promote your books on Instagram but do not know what to post. Read this to get content ideas for your book marketing.

75. Setup your Instagram Account

Instagram is a place where you can promote your book and interact with your fans.

76. Holiday Gift

A book can be promoted as a holiday gift item even though it may not be directly related to the holiday.

77. Prizes

Giveaways include necklaces, shirts, and tote bags with prizes for the author's name. These things stand out in the Instagram pictures.

78. Upcoming Books

Use Instagram to get people excited about your new books.

79. Showcase Special Events

People often post pictures of books on a table with a bunch of props or at events that have something to do with them.

80. Use Book Excerpts

You can show quotes and excerpts in beautiful pictures that your followers can not resist.

Choose your quotes carefully. Your words can get people interested in your book. If possible,

use videos to show your readers what went on behind the scenes to make your book.

81. Use Models to pose with your Brand

If you do not like being in front of the camera, you can pay models to pose with your book, product, or brand. Use relevant props so that it stands out in users' feeds.

82. Write to your Readers

Put up pictures of people reading your books without showing their faces. Another great idea for people who are shy in front of the camera

83. Use comments from Fans

You can ask people who like your book to take a picture of themselves reading it and send it to you.

84. Books as Gifts

Give some of your books as gifts and keep in touch with the people who read them. They can leave feedback on your Instagram feed.

85. Match your Book's Tone to its cover

Use creative props and lighting to give their Instagram posts a vintage or moody feel that goes with the books they are promoting.

86. Ask Questions

Ask your Instagram followers questions, sometimes in the picture itself and sometimes in the caption, to get them to interact with your posts.

87. Advertise on Instagram

Advertising lets you reach as many people as possible in a short time. People can interact with your post, making it more likely to appear in Instagram search results.

Millions of people use Instagram daily and tap the "Search" button. Your posts can start to show up higher in search results, especially when someone searches for keywords related to books.

88. Create an Author's Website

Businesses, authors, and small publishers can have professional-looking website that works on mobile devices. Invest in a high-quality website developer that can make your website attractive and responsive.

On your author's website, each book should have its page with a description. List all of your books on one page and then link to a separate page for each book using a "read more" link.

89. Domain Name Guide

People are more likely to search for your name, and putting all of your books on one site makes it easy for people looking for a specific book to find your other works. Even if you have only written one book and are a first-time author, it should still be yourname.com.

90. Pub-site

Website Pub-Site is a site that makes it easy for authors and publishers to create websites.

It has a free trial and a paid version for books, authors, and small publishers.

91. Send Visitors to your Book's Website

You can send visitors to the author's website by promoting and placing advertisements.

Sending traffic to your website can result in sales.

92. About the Author

Give both a short and a long bio about the author. Again, when people go to that page, they want to know more. The short bio could go on the home page with a link to the full bio that says "read more."

93. Link to Book Sellers

Include links to stores such as:

Amazon

Barnes & Noble

Indie Bound (a network of hundreds of independent bookstores)

Books-A-Million

Apple iBooks

Indigo

Kobo

94. Media

Include author photos and book covers that people can download on your media page and links to your online coverage. Put a link to your contact page on your website so that the media can find it easy to contact or talk to you.

95. Free Books and Courses

Get people to visit your website, develop an interest in your brand, and sign up for your mailing list. You can also tell people about the giveaway through your mailing list.

96. Unique Visitors

The number of people who visit your site is not the same as the number of times they see it. So if Sam visits your site ten times, that is one unique visitor.

97. Page Views

As the number of page views increases, more people are on your author's website. You can see where people go on your website and how many pages they look at each time they go there.

98. Social Visits

Go to the Traffic Sources section of Google Analytics to find out which social media sites send the most people to your website. You will be able to see which sites send people to yours.

99. Customized Landing Page

You might want to make a special introduction for people who come to your website from your Twitter profile, Facebook fan page, Goodreads page, and more.

100. Share your Links

Share links to your new blog posts on all of the social media sites you use. But do not just post a link. Ask an exciting question, and provide an excerpt or explanation of why the post might interest people on that social network.

Landing Page Strategies

A landing page is a product information page where consumers can view a product, buy something or request additional information. Make your landing page easy for customers and the user interface attractive so readers can stay longer on your landing page.

101. Take Away the Menu Links

It is essential to keep your visitors' attention on one thing: making a purchase. Any other button or link to a different page can be a distraction.

102. Add Reviews to your Landing Page

People usually read reviews of a product to determine if the offer is worth it. I recommend putting customer reviews on your landing page.

103. Use Color Psychology

Ensure the person who produces your landing page pays attention to the colors and that they match your logo, website, and other marketing materials.

104. Copywriting

Use clear, simple language to quickly and clearly explain the offer's value. Explain what you are offering to the audience. Ensure the content is easy to read.

Many people who read Website content do so quickly; bullet points, lists, and different font sizes make it easy to read.

105. Add a picture of yourself, a product, or a business to Your Landing Page

It works better when you show your face or the faces of your team or customers who are happy. Most case studies show that pictures of real people increase conversion rates.

106. Add a Video to your Landing Page

A video can help you connect with viewers and teach them how your brand can help them.

107. Prove Your Credibility

Show that your product or service is trustworthy by displaying awards, honors, or other credentials you have acquired.

108. Include Your Contact Information

Show the name of your company or business, your contact information, and a Google map of your location.

109. Add Buttons for Social Sharing

Google "likes" pages are often shared, so use social buttons to encourage people to share your content.

110. Test Your Landing Page

It is a way to compare two versions of the same variable, usually by seeing how a subject reacts to each one.

Pick A Landing page Design That Works Well On Mobile Devices. Some observations say more traffic is on mobile devices than desktop computers.

111. Add Value

Your landing page needs to show that it has value beyond just meeting needs.

112. Use Figures

Concrete numbers and values from the real world are much more convincing than general numbers. Tell them how much in figures your brand is likely to change how they think.

Influencer Marketing

A person with authority and popularity in a specific niche is called an influencer. Influencers have large audiences who care about what they say, like, and suggest. Our daily lives are full of information, noise, and alerts. So, one easy way to sort through them is to listen to the advice of people you trust, such as people with much influence.

A recommendation from a book influencer is a form of social proof for a book and can have a natural effect on book sales and awareness of you as an author.

113. Consider Values when choosing Influencers

As an author, find an influencer to work with, whose values and goals are similar to yours.

People will remember that you worked with that influential person long after the campaign.

114. Seek Genuineness

An influencer who is active and generates genuine interest can yield fruitful results.

115. Pick one that fits your budget

There are many influencers with anywhere from a few thousand to millions of followers. You might consider one that you can afford.

116. Think about reach and goals

Reach is how many people you might be able to engage with through the influencers. Remember that a small audience can be helpful and help you reach your goals.

117. Allow time for review

Give the reviewer access to your product, service, course, or book. They risk their reputations by providing a review.

118. Uphold Your Values

Tell your influencer what you believe is essential to you so your audience will understand your core values.

119. Prepare the Perfect Pitch

For example, an author is likely to work with an influencer who posts about reading and books.

Influencers want to keep their audience interested, and it is up to you to show them how working with you will do that.

120. Set up offers

Consider giving them an exclusive chance to tell their readers about your book. Influencers love it when they can provide their fans with things, they cannot get anywhere else.

121. Manage Influencers

Influencers work with various people and businesses. To effectively manage influencers, try to understand their needs and type of audience.

122. Promotional Tools

You could give people gifts like pens, cups, blankets, or bottles with the book's cover printed on them.

123. Optimized Content

Ensure your influencers do not miss relevant keywords by giving them your content that is optimized.

124. Research

Many celebrities and influencers have their email addresses and other contact information on their websites.

Check out what your potential influencers are posting on social media. How often do they share content? If they already send many paid posts to their followers, their engagement rate might not last. Look for natural, free content to keep your followers interested, excited, and involved.

125. Measure the Impact

When you start your influencer campaign, it can be tempting to measure things like likes and comments instead of your sales.

Webinar

Webinar marketing is an affordable method of talking to people interested in your product or service online in real-time. You can keep talking to them and moving them through the sales cycle to make them customers. You can promote your book through webinars as part of a marketing strategy.

126. Educate people

Webinars are great ways to educate people on your new product or service.

127. Exposure

Use a webinar to show your product or service to potential clients or customers.

128. Sales

You can also meet with your sales reps and agents to show them your new catalog, new products, books, and new sales ideas, or send them a video or a link to your webinar.

129. Webinar Replays & Income

With an evergreen webinar system, once you record a webinar, you can repeatedly sell the content from that webinar.

130. Benefits of Webinars

Once you start webinars, you will quickly build a group of people looking forward to each one.

You can talk to hundreds of potential customers all at once.

131. Launch with a Webinar or Video

Businesses can sell their new products by creating a webinar or video and sharing them on social media. Webinars are much more exciting and valuable than sales pages.

132. Save Sales Time

With webinars, you can make sales faster than with many other ways to market. You can generate sales with up to a one-hour webinar or video.

133. Demonstrate & Showcase

You can coach your clients one at a time or in groups using webinars, which is faster than making phone calls. A video is also very helpful.

134. Make Videos from Webinars

Webinars make it easy to make new videos you can share on YouTube, Facebook, and other sites. Videos are great for showing people a new product, service, training course, or book.

135. Live Webinar Interviews

Interviewing influential people in your field in a live webinar is one of the best ways to get to know them and build relationships. You can have a webinar anywhere and at any time. You might need to prepare your scripts ahead of time.

136. Interesting Topic

Getting people to sign up for a webinar is easy if the topic is something exciting. Many people show interest when watching a video, webinar, or invention.

137. Keep Your Promises

During webinars, it is common for customers to ask questions. Remember to do so when you promise to send a link after the session.

138. Informed Consumers

You can inform, educate, and entertain consumers, before they buy anything from you.

139. Conversion

Once you know how to run webinars well, it is easy to convert more attendees.

140. Promote

Once you set up the webinar, tell everyone you know about it. You could inform your subscribers first, and you can also ask them to share the news.

141. Webinars, Easy to Navigate

Most webinar platforms allow users to pause, play, rewind, or fast forward. Ensure your webinar has the option for easy navigation so your listeners can watch at their pace

142. User Generated Content

User-generated content is the content that users of a brand generate on their own. Many companies make user-generated content an essential part of their sales promotional strategies. It could be anything, like comments, reviews, pictures, or posts on social media.

To use user-generated content in your advertising, you should ask for permission from your audience. Using this accurate content on platforms other than social media can help you get people's attention.

143. Build Anticipation

It can be tempting to run your campaigns for user-generated content for weeks or even months. Instead, think about planning your campaign around a specific date and building up to the big event.

144. Provide Tools

Use tools to make participating in your campaign easy and fun for people. These could be as simple as quotes that make them feel good that they can tweet.

145. Behind the Scene

User-generated content does not always come from fans; it can also come from official influencers. Think about photos and other unique content from the launch of a product, book, or other brand events.

146. Engage with Audience

Once your user-generated campaign runs, thank your readers and say nice things about what they sent. You could also start a conversation to keep the engagement going.

147. Reach New Audiences

You can create a broader reach by promoting your Brand, both online and offline, at live events, and in print. You can effectively reach new audiences by bringing social content to new sites and platforms.

148. A Challenging and Rewarding Task

Create a challenge or contest to get people excited and a chance to get a reward.

149. Use Relevant Keywords

When people search for terms that are very relevant to you, your books, or your site, search engines like Google should bring up your site.

150. Words That Fit Your Book's Category

Using keywords related to your Brand to rank higher on search engines would be great.

151. Use Guest Posts

When you post as a guest on other sites, you get the chance to link back to your site.

152. Use Good Pictures

Visuals catch our attention and hold it; images can attract your readers.

153. Thank Other Bloggers

When other writers, bloggers, or influential people link your site, a simple thank you to them will go a long way.

154. Content Calendar

Making a content calendar is the best way to make the most of the limited time spent "building an online presence." By planning a few weeks of blog post ideas at once, you may not spend much time wondering what to write.

155. Post Content on LinkedIn

By posting content on LinkedIn, you can get more traffic and raise your profile in your field. Join groups for your book's category, give good advice, ask good questions, and talk about your thoughts.

156. Google Alerts

Your business name, website, and the name of your books on Google Alerts can help you track who is blogging about you.

157. Include Share Links

Most times, your readers know someone that will find your content helpful. Always include a link that will make those that read your content share it.

Forum Marketing

Using forums to market your book is a great way to get it out to the public. Most forum users know how to use the Internet and are ready to make online purchases. Many forum users are also well-known experts and bloggers on the topics the forum covers.

158. Respect the rules of the Forum

While signing up, you may agree to the forum's user agreement and posting rules. Learn very carefully about these kinds of restrictions and policies.

Understand the rules and how the forums work so you do not find yourself breaking the rules.

You can also create forums within social media groups or your website related to the content of your book.

159. Focus On Your Specialty

For forum marketing to be helpful, you can search to find the right community. Look for public forums where people talk about your niche.

160. Use Google

Use the largest search engine to find forums for your Brand.

161. Prepare Your Books

When you find forums that you want to use for online marketing, you will need to set up your forum account right away.

162. Name of User

Your user name is the first thing other people who use the site will notice about you. Pick a username that shows what you do.

163. Who You Are

A high profile can help someone show that they can trust the forum. Feel free to add personal information to make your profile more interesting.

164. First Post

Your first post could include a summary of your experience, achievements, what you know, and information about why you joined the forum. Let some of your other customers know that your main goal is to get involved in the community and learn from it.

165. Do not try to sell with First Post

In your first post, introduce yourself and comment on other people's posts. Some sites have a policy against trying to generate sales on the first post.

Remember that it is about joining the community, being helpful, and even adding something of value.

166. Avoid Argument

People stay and talk on the forum, and there may be disagreements. Do not try to pick a side; instead, remain neutral and keep a positive tone.

167. Create a Link

Make a signature with links that will show up at the bottom of your posts. You can sign your posts with this. This signature needs to take people to your website. The traffic you get from it could be very well-suited to what you want.

168. Start a Thread

Make interesting threads about what is "hot" right now. You can make a step-by-step guide to your solution in the form of a line from your book.

169. Answer Questions

Answer current topics with good answers. Look for questions that people have asked because they want to learn more. Give an excellent response to the question. Your audience will regard you as an expert and respects your opinions when you do this.

170. Track Forums

You cannot participate in every forum, so keep track of the ones you use and stick with them.

171. Find Your Audience

Find forums where your customers are regularly talking with each other.

172. Paid Sponsor

Send the site's owner or head administrator a private message explaining your product and request to become a paid sponsor.

173. Respond to Criticism

Respond as soon as possible to complaints and criticisms, and do not take them personally. Handle the issue without attacking anyone's personality

174. Maintain Relevance

Get people to come to you for answers about your niche. You might even turn some people who use your forum into customers for life.

Selling to Book Stores

It is possible to sell to Independent bookstores and other retailers.

175. Start by Being a Client.

Build relationships with bookstores by buying books from them and telling your friends, family, and fans to do the same.

176. Research the bookstore

Check out the store's social media to see the author events they usually put on. Use this information in your pitch when you meet with the owner. Mention that you are available to answer any questions from people interested in your Brand.

177. Contact Librarians or Buyers

You can send a mail or an email to the librarians or buyers and provide them with information about your book.

178. Explain Your Brand

A store owner will want to know that your book is something their customers will like. Be able to explain what your book is about clearly and briefly.

179. Return Policies

Make purchasing your book or product user-friendly by instituting a return policy that makes people feel comfortable purchasing.

180. Your Best Book

By putting your best book forward, you can earn credibility and trust from your viewers.

181. Packaging

Books that stand out for the wrong reasons do not interest booksellers. Visit a bookstore near you and take note of the trim sizes, images on the book covers, and the insides.

182. Appealing Book Cover

Make your book cover appealing and irresistible so that it wins the space on the shelf.

183. Industry Standards

Your book can be different from everyone else's, but when you notice recurring themes in specific categories, stick with them because they are probably industry standards.

184. Pricing

Your book or product should have a reasonable price that users can afford.

Do you know how much your book or product should cost? Our research indicates that running ads for books or products that have affordable prices could lead to more sales.

185. Use a Reputable Distributor

The bookstore will find it easier to sell your book when you use a reputable distributor. The easier it is for a bookstore to sell your book, the more likely they will try.

186. Create a Plan

The store wants to sell your book, but do not expect them to do all the work for you. Have a good plan for marketing your book.

187. Go to Where Bookstores Buy Books

Independent bookstores buy books from wholesalers and sometimes from authors or publishers directly.

188. Explore

Your book could be an excellent fit for thousands of libraries and bookstores. Research your market to find various options.

189. Book Spine

You will always need to make an excellent cover for your book. You could pay attention to your spine to sell in bookstores. Remember that most bookstores only show the spines of books.

190. The blurb or a Brief Description

The blurb makes a reader want to buy your book and take it home. Misspellings or grammar problems are unacceptable. This short and brief writing should be professional.

191. Book cover Imprinted on Gift Items

Customers will generate interest and excitement in your book or product if you give them promotional items such as a mug or shirt with the book's cover. Give gifts at book events and trade shows.

Book Event

Book events are unique ways to sell books to readers.

Events help you sell books and give you information about what readers think of your book.

192. Sign Up Early

One way to sell books is to sign up as soon as possible for the book event. Signing up and arriving early gives you more time to market and promote your book before the event.

193. Promote the Book Event

Now that you have signed up, tell people about your book and how they can contact you.

194. Bring Necessary Items

Remember to bring some things customers need, such as the book, the bookstand, and promotional items.

Have bookmarkers, stickers, pins, and pens to help spread the word about your book.

195. Stunning Display Table

Most book events have plain, open tables where you can display your books and other items.

196. Bring Many Books to Events

Bring as many books as possible, between 25 and 50, to a book signing and other promotional events.

197. Keep in Touch

Always get the customer's information so you can contact them later and answer any questions they may have. You should be in a good mood when you go to book events and enjoy talking to readers and connecting with other authors.

198. Engage

Take the initiative to promote sales at book events by offering discounts and other incentives. Do not just sit behind the pile of books and wait for people to come to your table.

Get up and talk to the people about your book to get them interested.

199. Variety of Formats

Having your books available in text, eBook, digital and audio formats gives the audience a variety to choose from and could lead to more sales.

200. Plan a Talk

Plan to give a talk instead of a book signing, no matter where the event is. People are more interested in a conversation than an author sitting at a table.

201. Create Attention

Consider doing events in unique places. You can do them in restaurants, gyms, video stores, and electronics stores.

202. Negotiation

Customers like to be in charge, so let them negotiate and choose what works for them.

203. Offer Bundles

People love deals, so if you have written more than one book, you might offer a discount when someone buys more than one.

204. Your Other Services

As an option at your sales table, inform the audience of other services you offer, such as coaching or consulting. Make an order form that lists all of your books, bundles, and consulting services.

205. Plan to take pictures

People will often ask to take a picture with you. Do not let this surprise you.

206. Guest Posting & Virtual Book Tours

Guest posting means writing content for the website or blog of another company. Guest bloggers usually write blogs on websites that are similar to theirs.

Guest blogging can be helpful to your host, their audience, and you as the blogger. is pre-recorded on video and which you can send to your audience as a follow-up.

207. Pick an Important Topic for a Blog Post

Make it about what the people who visit your site want, not what you want. If it does not appeal to the people who read your host's blog, they may not read it. Do not write something quickly and send it without thinking about what you want to say. Edit and proofread it. The host will accept a well-written post.

208. Only Guest Blogs on Relevant Sites

You should only write blogs to help you reach your goal and stay true to your brand's values.

209. Writing for Other Sites

Just as publicity leads to more promotions, writing great guest posts will help you get invited to write for other sites your audience visits.

210. Expert in Your Niche

When people who might be interested in your niche see you posting valuable and fun content on popular sites, it is easy for them to think of you as an expert in your field.

211. Use Your Content in The Right Way

When you write a guest post for a popular site, many people who are active in the community will read it.

212. Feature in Media Outlet

When you are in the media, people who want to buy your book often write down your name, then remember to look you up online, find your information, and buy your book. You can simplify the purchasing process by providing your contact information to people.

213. Write to bloggers

By giving famous bloggers a guest post, you are giving them something valuable instead of asking for a favor to review your book.

214. Start with Smaller Sites

You want to find blogs with a good-sized audience and have earned the trust of their readers. Use your best judgment, and do not write off all smaller sites, especially when starting with guest blogging.

215. Make Your Pitch

Send the blogger an email or use the blog's contact form to send three to five ideas for blog posts. During this step, follow the writer's instructions and send in your suggestions as they ask.

216. Follow Up on Posts

If the post does well and leads to many book sales or sign-ups, reach out to the blogger and ask if you can write for them again. Build long-term relationships with blogs that get much traffic and become a regular contributor if possible.

217. Thank Your Host

No blog post is complete without a shout-out to the person who was so kind to let you post on their blog.

218. Discuss Your Book

Connect the author's real story to the story of the book. Use a transition to add a summary of your book to your blog post.

219. Keep it Brief

Most book bloggers have word counts they think are best.

220. Measure Result

Has guest blogging on your website been helpful for you? Do people seem to be interested in what you write? Do you have a possible buyer's attention? These are the questions you ask to see how far you have come.

221. Promote the website you guest posted on

Place the link to the website on your social media handles so your audience can see some of your content as they visit the site.

Email Newsletter

Some forms of communication are short and easy to share, like posts on social media. Email newsletters can be effective in connecting with clients.

Most people get emails daily, so you could write your email newsletters to target your market and catch the reader's attention.

222. Value only

One way to improve your marketing content is to test its value with your most exciting audience before you spend time and money making it.

223. Images

People have been sending out newsletters for a long time. Many businesses and professionals have newsletters, so you need to do a few things to make yours stand out. Use pictures and videos because they are easier to understand and often more fun to watch.

224. Show the Culture of Your Brand

Use your content to show what your Brand stands for and what makes it great.

225. Subject Line of Emails

The subject line of your email must be an exciting topic. To get people to open your emails, you must first get their attention with your subject line.

226. Eye-Catching Headlines

No matter how attractive the rest of your email is, the headline should be appealing and exciting for people to read. You can divide your clients into segments and send them relevant information with different headlines.

227. Use Stories

Personal or business-related stories can draw the readers' attention. By making them curious, you can get more people to open and respond to your emails, leading to more engagement and, in the end, more profitable email campaigns.

228. Add Video Link to Email Newsletters

Although you cannot play a video in an email, you can put a beautiful thumbnail with a tempting play button or a link to the video.

229. Easy-to-Understand Posts

Keep your messages as straightforward as possible. Every second of every hour, hundreds of brands and activities are trying to get your client's attention, so your post should be short, clear, and easy to understand.

230. Talk about Yourself & Your Brand

Email newsletters enable your clients to know you better.

231. Authenticity

Customers show interest in newsletters that are authentic and offer something of value every time.

232. Use Data to Evaluate

Use measurable data from keyword research, consumer insights, and product and customer care insights. Then, you can use these data inputs to get ideas for your email content.

233. Provide Ideas

Instead of telling your audience things they already know, give them ideas and insights people can use. Ask yourself if you would like to read it before sending it out.

234. Focus on Your Goals

Have clear goals, figure out what will interest your audience, and set clear key performance indicators.

235. Brand Your Emails

You can put your logo on it, and you might also put the same photo that you can use on social media accounts. That will help people recognize you and your brand.

Collect mail and email addresses for future promotions of your business. When you create a newsletter, these addresses will be helpful.

236. Web-safe Fonts

First, email newsletters look different on web browsers, so the best way to make them look the same everywhere is to use web-safe fonts.

237. Colors

Your brand, logo, and color should be consistent with each other. In the body of your newsletter, you could change the colors of images to reflect the season, such as Thanksgiving and Christmas.

238. Call To Action Colors

You can try different images, colors, and talk to your designer to determine which color works best for your subscribers.

A call to action should be clear, direct, and require urgency. Do not ask people to do more than one thing at a time.

Book/Product Reviews

Positive reviews tell people that your product is worth their time and give you instant credibility. Authors that sell their books and courses know how to use their book reviews as an exceptional marketing tool.

239. Get Some Reviews

Almost no book will sell without at least a few reviews, and ten or twenty would be better. You should get some reviews before you spend money on ads. Choose the kind of review to help you reach your goals the best.

240. Get Help from Experts

Professional editors won't hold back when they tell you what works and needs to be changed. Just this is why you hire them.

241. Friends and family

Do not ask a friend to review your book because they love you and will not be able to tell you the truth about it. Instead, ask someone who will tell you the truth no matter what.

242. Put the Right Label on It

Book review editors need to know the book's category to find the right reviewer. Some authors who publish their books put the wrong book category and title on them. For example, some writers call it a mystery when it is a thriller or fiction when it is romance.

243. Reviewer

A professional review allows readers to know that the reviewers know much about the book.

244. Add Reviews to the back of the book

When your book gets good professional reviews, put some of these reviews on the front or back cover.

245. Follow Up With Reviewers

Some reviewers will focus on a topic that is important to them but not your market. Contact those reviewers and ask them for more information.

246. Answer the Reviews

Regarding communication, reviews can help your company and its customers post comments and engage with each other.

Put customer reviews in your pricing packages to show that your products or services have positive reviews.

247. More Reviews

One good review is fine, but better to have three or four. Use your first review to get more reviews. Tell other reviewers that X has reviewed your product and you would like them to do the same.

248. Your Online Site

At the top of your author's Website, there should be a tab called "Book Reviews" that leads to excerpts or product reviews.

249. Copy Editor

Use a good editor to edit your book professionally. Copyediting is a skill that takes someone who knows a lot about books to do well.

250. Social Media

Reviews are good things to talk about on social media. For example, posting a review on your Facebook page is another way to tell your friends about your new book.

251. Get The Word Out

When contacting bloggers, major news outlets, bookstores, and librarians about your book, it is helpful to send them a press release about it. At the top of the press release, a quote from a professional review will catch their attention.

252. Marketing Materials

Use a quote from a good review on postcards, bookmarks, information sheets, shelf talkers, and other marketing materials to let people know about book signings or other events.

253. Sell to Booksellers

Booksellers and distributors may not read every book that comes into their offices. Instead, they rely on reviews to find good books for their customers.

254. Book Description

You can use these great reviews anywhere you need to describe your book, and you could sell more copies.

When someone does click on your book description, you want them to keep reading. Does it attract attention? Are the most potent emotional hooks in the first few sentences? Try to get your audience to buy your book at every turn.

255. Use Feedback to Get Better

Do not give up when a review is not as good as you had hoped.

Put aside a poor product review while you think about it. Then reread it with as little bias as possible and consider what the reviewer said.

Getting feedback from a third party is never a waste of time.

Free Book Promotion Sites

Book promotion sites can be a great way to get your book in front of new readers, which is why some authors use free and paid book promotion services. Finding sites to promote on and determine their needs can take time.

256. All Authors

With the free option, you can have a basic author page, be listed in the Author Directory, and add up to four books. Additional information and specific up-to-date requirements are on its website.

257. Authors' Den

A basic account is free, but you pay to become a "gold" member and get more attention. Additional information and specific up-to-date requirements are on its website.

258. Awesome Gang

Access to one of the best email lists of free books. Additional information and specific up-to-date requirements are on its website.

259. Book Hunt

Start sharing your book and get votes in favor of it. The more people like your book, the more they share their views. Additional information and specific up-to-date requirements are on its website.

260. Book Praiser

Create an account for free. It allows you to make an author page on the site to show off more of your work. Additional information and specific up-to-date requirements are on its website.

261. Free Book Tips

You can send your book anytime to Free Book Tips. Additional information and specific up-to-date requirements are on its website.

262. Indies Today

Books should be accessible for Indies Today. Additional information and specific up-to-date requirements are on its website.

263. Inkitt

The company can send information about your book to thousands of readers. Additional information and specific up-to-date requirements are on its website.

264. Free Stuff

As its name suggests, it gives away many things for free, not just ebooks. Additional information and specific up-to-date requirements are on its website.

265. Kindle Book Review

Information and specific up-to-date requirements are on its website.

266. Indie Author News

It welcomes fiction and nonfiction. You can get the tag "author of the day" and gain more exposure. Additional information and specific up-to-date requirements are on its website.

267. Lovely Book Promotions

For paid promotions, the company will promote to several Facebook groups. Additional information and specific up-to-date requirements are on its website.

268. Topless Cowboy

It caters to cowboy and western romance. Additional information and specific up-to-date requirements are on its website.

269. Reading Deals

Information and specific up-to-date requirements are on its website.

270. Best Book Monkey

The paid option on Best Book Monkey gives readers a spot in the daily newsletter. Additional information and specific up-to-date requirements are on its website.

271. Book Angel

It can only have PG-13 content and promotes free and discounted ebooks. Additional information and specific up-to-date requirements are on its website.

272. Digital Book Today

A 4+ average review score is required. Additional information and specific up-to-date requirements are on its website.

Paid Book Promotion Sites

While you can begin with the free book promotion sites, you can eventually upgrade to the paid version to acquire more significant exposure for your book and ultimately increase sales!

After you have tried the accessible version of your book promotion sites, depending on what your decision is, you can choose to upgrade to the paid version.

Below, we are providing just the names of paid promotional websites (except for three, which have additional information).

Additional information and specific up-to-date requirements are on each company's website.

273. Independent Author Network

274. Author Ad Network

275. Bargain Booksy

276. Book Adrenaline

277. BookBub

It helps people discover new books and authors.

278. Book Cave

279. Book Gorilla

It promotes best sellers, other discounted books, and ebooks.

280. Book Tweeters

It Tweets information on books to thousands of viewers.

281. Book Doggy

282. Book Melon

283. BookRaid

284. Book Sliced

285. Crave Books

286. Dango Books

287. eBook Hounds

288. eBook Soda

289. Freebooksy

Press Release

It can create excitement when you use a press release to market your book. It is not a common way to promote sales. It but it can generate additional sales leads and inquiries.

A book press release is also a way to show off your book in an interesting way to journalists and news organizations.

290. Distribute the Press Release

Send your press release to news reporters who can spread the word about your book. Use a professional syndication service like eReleases.

291. Audience

Once you know who your press release is for, you will be able to write it in a way that gets people's attention.

292. The headline of the Press Release

The main idea is to write a headline that makes people want to keep reading. People will notice a press release that stands out with a great heading

293. Subheading

Some press releases have subheadings, while others do not.

Include the date and where you are at the time of writing for your audience to know how recent the release is.

294. Format

Next, set up the correct format, structure, and font for the press release (e.g., Times New Roman, 12pt). Journalists and media outlets will expect the standard press release format to ensure that more people will read it.

295. Good Starting Point

You might want to start with something that gets people's attention, like a controversial statement or a sentence that makes people feel something about the book you are promoting.

296. Your background

Tell your audience about your background as an author, the number of books you have written, and any awards.

297. Relevant Contact Details

The bare minimum is your email address, phone number, and website.

298. Keep it Simple

Use short, easy-to-understand sentences. People do not have time to look up your words in a dictionary.

299. Trendy Titles

Keep an eye out for new movies in your type of book and big hits on best-selling books. Again, the key is to go after the hottest new books so that yours shows up next to them.

300. Show off Products

You can target paperback versions of your competitor's books with Amazon's Product Display ads. Also, use relevant keywords for search engine optimization.

301. Nice Book Cover

Look at bestselling designs in your category. Also, spend money on a professional graphic designer to upgrade the quality of your book cover or promotional materials.

302. Follow Results

Your ad can get impressions by targeting your audience.

You can use automatic targeting, which will help you get more impressions, or do it manually.

303. Use Data

Set up a schedule for yourself to check on your progress at least once a week. Put information on an Excel sheet. Take note of which keywords lead to the most sales.

304. Keep up with the Times

Look at what people are trying to find. You can use Google Trends or Merchant Words, both free, to find keywords.

305. Cost

Your Cost Per Click (CPC) is another good number to monitor. It will enable you to determine your cost to acquire one customer. Let's assume that one out of every ten people who click on your ad, buys your book. A cost per click of $.50 means that each time someone buys your book, it costs approximately $5 on the advertising platform. A higher conversion rate will lower the advertising cost.

306. Rate of Click-through

You can improve your click-through rate by updating your packaging, changing your cover and the first sentences of your blurb, and adding a link to your Amazon author page.

307. Invite Family and Friends

Share your book link on Amazon and encourage family and friends to buy it.

Goodreads

Goodreads is a vast database of books with several active customer forums and groups.

It allows showing your book to thousands of people who might not have found you or your book otherwise.

308. Sign up

Go to the Goodreads website to sign up for an Account and start promoting your book.

309. Read other books in Your Area of Specialty

Avoid writing something similar to other books in your category by reading those books and researching your target market. When you know what is out there, you can write a book that fits your audience's needs without making a story that seems too familiar. People believe other readers. Start adding books you would like to read.

310. Timing

Your giveaway can happen at least 30 days before your launch. For 30 days, your giveaway could be the only way for people to get a copy of your book before it comes out.

311. Ask Fans for Review

A book displays on Goodreads based on how many reviews it has.

312. Giveaway on Goodreads

There are contests where readers can try to win free books. In these giveaways, authors and publishers can give away books for free as prizes. You can offer one book or more than one.

313. Add Your Book to Lists

Lists are still a great way to get your book in front of readers who might not have found it otherwise.

314. Goodreads Forums

Use the Goodreads forums for your type of book and start interacting with readers who like the kind of books you write.

315. Add a link to the Website

Add a feature from Goodreads to your website. From there, people can click to go to your Goodreads profile.

316. Connect to Your Goodreads Account

Connect your Facebook account to your Goodreads account so that what you do on Goodreads will appear on Facebook.

317. Review Books

When you rate and review a book, it is easier for other readers to find and get in touch with you. Also, you can discover new books through reviews.

318. Questions and Answers with the Author

The first is Ask the Author, on Goodreads, which you can set up in your author profile. These questions are on your author profile and allow you to communicate with your readers.

319. Complete Your Profile

Add an engaging description and a professional photo to your profile, and avoid leaving out important information.

320. Synchronize

Goodreads lets authors blog on their site, but it is better to sync your blog to them from your author's website.

321. Goodreads Polls

Use author-centered questions or polls to find out what people are looking for in a book or how they feel about yours.

322. Quiz

Quizzes are a fun way to give your fans and readers something to do and can help spread the word about your book.

323. Quotes

You are the proud author of a book, and you can add your quote to Goodreads.

324. Promote Events in Goodreads Profile

You can use Goodreads to spread the word about a book signing, a talk, or a presentation at a conference. Your profile will show the events.

Affiliate Marketing

It is a system that incentivizes partners to promote your products in exchange for a commission. A customer, advocate, or marketer in your industry joins your affiliate program and sends people to your products through a unique link called an affiliate link.

325. Select Your Product

Decide which product you want to be part of your affiliate program.

326. Recruit Affiliates

Many businesses recruit affiliates from online promotional activities.

327. Manage Your Affiliates

Ensure your affiliates understand the program's rules and know your Brand. Making a stock of content they can use, like tutorials, webinars, and graphics is a good idea.

328. Collaborate with A Brand Similar to Yours

When collaborating with another business, ensure you can reach the same or similar audience. If not, the promotion may not get much attention.

329. Let Your Brands Stand Out

Have a robust product identity so that affiliates can promote your product or services satisfactorily. Promote your brands and make them easily identifiable by people.

330. Tell your Partners

An affiliate's blog that gets a good number of visitors could help promote your post to the visitors.

331. Check Your Progress as You Go

Without measurable goals, it can be hard to tell your affiliate program's success. Keep working on it to ensure it gives you a good return on your time.

332. Place Your Affiliates in Key Spots

You could place affiliates strategically to help the sales process proceed efficiently.

333. Utilize Affiliates on Social Media

Have your marketers promote you on social media platforms, and let them interact with customers who can upgrade your Brand or write reviews.

334. Affiliate Incentives

Consider giving commission bonuses to your best affiliates who meet their target goals.

335. Use a Partner Network

An affiliate partner network can help you quickly build a base of representatives, especially if they already have relationships with other top affiliates in your industry.

336. Turn Your Club into A Network

The people in your book club, who are part of your closer audience, can become your affiliates quickly and easily because they already know what you do and can do it well.

337. Let Affiliates Use Your Product

You could even let them try out your products or services for free or at a lower price so they can write about you in a way that sounds realistic.

338. Expand Your Reach

You can target a geographical area where you can promote or advertise your Brand.

Use a combination of online and offline marketing to boost sales.

339. Introduce your Brand

Use flyers to get the word out, whether new to the market or trying to change your brand. Make flyers that show the cover of your book, the courses you teach, and what you do.

340. Add New Books and Courses

Use flyers to tell people who might buy your new product about it. Tell them what they will get out of using what you are selling.

341. Utilize Holiday Sales

Take advantage of every holiday to remind people about your business. Most likely, people spend money during the holidays. It pays to be in people's minds when they are ready to buy something.

342. Use Flyers to Promote an Event or Specials

There are many ways to get people to attend your event, class, or seminar. Flyers can help get the word out quickly. Use bright colors and images to describe the event.

When there is a community event, let people know you are there too. Give a discount on your books. Use them to get people to visit your store or use your other services.

343. Include Contact Information

Tell people how to reach you to get them to do something. Make business cards with your online and email addresses.

344. Inform & Educate

Share information to become a leader in your business field. Give helpful information about your books or courses to help your customers learn more about them.

345. Set Up Rewards & Coupons

Make a loyalty or referral program and hand out flyers to let people know about it, online or offline.

346. Display Flyers on Business Windows

In addition to leaving flyers in prominent places inside busy shops, salons, cafes, and restaurants, you can also ask the business owner to put your flyer in their display window.

347. Distribute to Mailboxes

Distributing your promotional materials to people's homes in their mailboxes is a popular and effective way to get people in your area interested in and buying your book. Distribute them with caution and courtesy.

348. Generate Leads

Flyers are a great way to bring in more potential customers. They are good at getting more people to know about your Brand and come to your store or buy your products.

349. Include Passages from Your Book

People who might buy your writing want to see a sample, especially if it is fiction. Use an analogy or short story to show your book's main point for a nonfiction book.

350. Uniqueness

When promoting offline with the use of business cards as an author, having a business card in the form of a book is a great way to make it stand out. Always show your business's primary product or service clearly and uniquely.

Chapter Eighteen

To All Our Valued Readers

Kindly Leave a Book Review

T HANK YOU FOR TAKING the time out of your busy schedules to read this book: "How To Promote Your Business & Increase Sales."

We are very grateful to you.

Kindly provide an honest, short, 2-sentence review for other readers to see.

Remember to include your first name, followed by the name of your business.

Kindly go to the site where you purchased this book, such as Amazon, enter the title of this book and scroll down to "leave a review."

Much appreciated. Thank you, from:

A2 Best Seller Publishers

Chapter Nineteen

Other Services We Provide

A2 Best Seller Publishers

Our Other Services:
Book Formatting, Editing,
Proof Reading, Cover Designs
Publishing & Marketing

FORMATTING YOUR BOOK; DONE for you

We can format your books professionally, both ebooks and print.

Proofreading and Editing; Done for You

Avoid costly grammatical or spelling errors. With our team of university graduates, we can look for plagiarism, make corrections as needed, and remove any duplicates.

Our capabilities include:

Writing Skills

Research Skills

Marketing Knowledge

Editing and Proofreading

End-of-Book Indexing of important topics throughout the book and their corresponding page numbers

(a service we can provide to other authors and publishers)

Book Publishing Services are available. Start the process by sending an email.

Thank you.

Chapter Twenty

Index

It starts on the next page.

Index

A

Action Words, 88
Adapt to changes, 53
Add reviews, 64
Add value, 13, 32
Add-ons, 116
Advertisements, 42, 47,
    87–88, 105
Advertisers, 16, 69
Advertising Budget, 81
Agency, 42, 80
Agreements, 80
All Authors, 185
Analyze, 21
Anniversary, 121
Announcements, 47
Apple, 9
Associates, 9, 59, 113
Author, 142, 151, 187–188,
    195

B

Balloons, 42
Billboards, 95
Billions, 8, 33–34
Birthday, 122
Blog, 10–11, 36, 113,
    118–119
Blogs, 8, 10–11, 19, 25,
    109, 118, 121, 129
Blurb, 171
Bonuses, 198
Booksellers, 184
Bookstores, 67, 170
Brand name, 28, 65
Branding, 17–19, 21, 23,
    25, 27, 29
Brands, 17, 102–103, 126,
    197
Broadcast, 119
Brochure, 61, 76, 88
Bryant University, 3
Budget, 21, 41, 50, 81
Bullet, 154
Bulletin boards, 59, 98
Business Cards, 44, 47,
    59–61, 117, 119
Business customers, 28–29
Business opportunities, 64
Businesspeople, 65
Buyer, 14, 71
Buyers, 45, 81, 103, 122,
    126

C

Calendar, 59, 164

Calls, 84, 108, 121, 123

Campaigns, 32, 55, 81, 84, 103, 119

Campus, 43

Capabilities, 64, 204

Captive Audience, 60

Catalogs, 74

Categories, 69

CDC, 1

Celebrities, 27, 42

Celebrity, 16

Charitable, 120

Chat, 140

Cheese, 47

Chef, 24

Church, 44

Circulars, 60

Click, 193

Client, 10, 12, 17–19, 44, 55, 57, 69, 112, 168

Clinics, 85

Clowns, 42

Club, 23, 74, 198

Cold emails, 55

Collaborate, 63, 65, 67, 69, 71, 115, 123, 197

Collaborate with Others, 63, 65, 67, 69, 71

College, 3, 43, 47

Comments, 11, 14, 18, 25, 34, 129–130, 149, 158

Commerce, 70–71

Commissions, 20, 110

Communicate, 8, 21, 25, 33, 52, 195

Community, 23, 41–42, 49, 108, 130

Competition, 10, 36, 63, 127

Competitors, 14, 21, 69, 71, 114

Complement, 69

Connections, 64, 134

Consideration, 2, 77

Consignee, 67–68

Consignment, 66–68

Consignor, 68

Consolidations, 122

Constant Contact, 57

Consultant, 66

Contests, 194

Copyright, 66

Core product, 64

Costco, 74

Costs, 39, 77–78, 82, 115, 121, 192

Countries, 39, 70

Coupons, 36, 41, 74, 77, 89, 120, 200

COVID-19, 1

Create demand, 102

Credit card companies, 73

Crowds, 41

Culture, 22, 31, 178

Curbside, 104
Curiosity, 124
Customer reviews, 14

D

Data, 179
Deals, 66, 106
Dedication, 1
Delay, 102
Delegate, 53
Deliveries, 104
Demand, 23, 26, 53, 77,
    102–103, 106
Demographic, 50
Dentists, 23, 73
Description, 24, 47, 49, 128
Design, 13
Designate, 16
Designer, 24
Desirable, 14
Digital marketing, 75
Directories, 37, 69
Directory, 68–69
Discuss, 13, 34, 110–111
Disease, 1
Display, 32, 43, 61, 74, 87,
    89, 104
Display Windows, 43
Distribution, 48, 51, 65, 77
Doctors, 1, 26
Dollars, 8, 29

E

Easter, 82
Ebay, 36
eBooks, 203
Economical, 88
Economy, 53
Email Lists, 58, 121, 185
Email Newsletters, 55–57
Enforcement, 26
Engage, 8, 11, 25, 34–35,
    61, 110, 117, 129
Engagement, 16, 74
Entrepreneur, 52–53, 108
Envelope, 76
Example, 9, 12–15, 18,
    23–24, 26, 73, 75, 77
Excellent, 9, 17, 20–22,
    28, 59
Excellent Customer Service,
    9, 17, 21–22
Exciting, 76
Expensive, 79, 82
Exposure, 16

F

Fabulous, 89
Facebook, 33
Feedback, 12–14
Flyers, 59–61
Focus, 75
Follow, 22–23, 71, 74, 76
Followers, 16

Food, 12, 18, 25, 42, 73, 87, 89
Food delivery services, 73
Forum, 13
Franchise, 65–66
Franchise consultant, 66
Franchisee, 65–66
Franchisor, 65
Frequent, 14, 73
Friendly, 24
Friends, 27, 44, 47, 64
Fundraisers, 130
Fundraising, 29, 85

G

Goodwill, 28, 107, 120, 122, 130
Google, 36
Governments, 8, 70
Grand Opening Events, 41
Greetings, 1
Groceries, 116
Group, 8, 18, 110–111, 121
Groups, 33, 63–64, 85, 110–111, 120
Guarantee, 126–127

H

Headline, 24, 55, 147, 190
Healthcare, 1, 26
Holiday, 45–47, 81, 116–117, 128
Holiday Promotions, 45

Holiday Sales, 45–46, 128
Holidays, 41, 43, 45–47, 49, 51, 53, 128
Host, 102, 140, 176
Hotmail, 4
Households, 83
Hybrid, 113

I

Ice Cream, 43–44
Images, 32, 61–62, 124
Impulse, 115–116
Income, 11, 50, 80, 85, 159
Independent, 86, 104, 188
Individuals, 20, 36, 50, 67, 75, 83, 110
Instagram, 12, 35
Internet, 2, 4–5, 7–8, 26–27, 37, 39, 68, 73, 84, 124
Interviews, 12, 160
Introductory letter, 76
invitations, 42, 135
Invite, 42, 122, 132, 193
Invoice, 85
Issuewire, 48

K

Keywords, 15
Kobo, 152

L

Landing, 36, 64
Language, 76
Laptops, 56
Launch, 12, 47, 75, 128, 130, 160
Lead generation, 85
Librarians, 169
LinkedIn, 34, 132–133, 164
Lists, 58, 91, 93, 121, 174, 185, 194
Live streams, 34, 121
Locations, 9, 25, 42, 60, 65, 76, 136
Lockdown, 2
Logo, 17, 20–21, 28–29
Lovely, 89, 126

M

Magazines, 74, 83, 87
Mailing List, 74
Mailings, 47, 73–74
Maintain, 13, 15, 56, 111–112, 168
Manage, 103
Market, 7–8, 56, 60, 63, 75, 77, 86
Marketers, 16
Medium, 27, 49, 51, 87
Meetings, 8, 28, 108, 117
Members, 24, 44, 126
Mergers, 122

Message, 47, 52, 55–56, 60, 75, 80, 108
Messages, 8, 35, 59, 102
Messaging, 8, 17, 32, 121
Millions, 1, 4, 15–16, 35, 150, 157
Minimize, 88
Minimum, 191
Mobile, 32–33, 130, 150, 155
Model, 68
Momentum, 32
Money, 35, 68, 118, 120, 126, 128
Monitor, 103, 137
Music, 41
Mystery, 114

N

Nationwide, 70
Native, 32–33
Neighborhoods, 76
Network, 63, 65, 67, 69, 71
New Accounts, 101
New Businesses, 28, 41, 60, 88
News Release, 49
Newsletter, 10, 56
Newspaper, 49, 87–89
Newsworthy, 49
Nurses, 1, 26

O

Occasion, 43
Online event, 120, 123
Online presentations, 28, 103
Online Sales, 10, 26
Online Shopping, 8
Optimization, 15–16
Orders, 9, 87, 126, 128
Overseas, 70–71, 109

P

Packages, 14
Pandemic, 1, 25–26, 104
Partners, 197
Patents, 66
Payments, 85
Photograph, 48–49, 128
Pictures, 61, 132, 163, 174
Pizza, 73
Pizza restaurants, 73
Podcasts, 8, 12, 19, 32, 103, 121
Politicians, 73
Positive Attitude, 52
Positive reviews, 14
Postcards, 73–76
Professional, 15, 29, 42, 52, 59, 63, 118
Publications, 87–88
Publicity, 41, 43, 49, 109

Q

Quality, 8, 10–11, 17, 31, 61, 77

R

Radio, 12, 79, 81, 122
Readers, 11, 27, 88, 202
Recipients, 55, 76
Reciprocate, 115
Recordings, 12
Recruit, 104
Referrals, 44, 47, 75, 106–107
Register, 28, 37, 48, 56, 116
Relationship, 12, 55
Release, 47–49, 130
Replay, 121
Repost, 109, 129
Representatives, 83–85, 107–108
Reps, 83–85
Research, 8, 24, 80–81, 86–87, 105, 204
Restaurants, 73, 104
Retailers, 9–10, 28, 46, 73, 84, 127
Retain, 2, 6, 102, 118
Reviews, 14, 18, 22, 24, 64, 115, 118, 120, 130
Rewards, 105
Risk, 65

Royalties, 66

S

Sale, 41, 46, 75, 115, 123, 128
Salespeople, 9
Salespersons, 84
Samples, 118
Satisfaction, 9, 15
Scarcity, 126
Scientists, 1
Search engines, 15, 19, 32, 68, 112–113
Seller, 68, 202–203
Selling to businesses, 83–84
SEO, 15, 24
Service Businesses, 28, 42, 47, 87, 89
Shipping, 46
Shoestring, 88
Shopify, 24
Shortages, 26
Showcase, 48, 62, 119, 133, 148, 160
Sidewalk signs, 97
Sign, 128
Sponsored, 16, 33
Squarespace, 11
Staples, 9
Strategist, 32
Strong brand, 19
Subject, 178
Subordinates, 53

Subscriptions, 11, 83
Success, 9, 22, 50, 52, 77, 119
Sundays, 88
Supermarkets, 59
Superstore, 9
Supply, 26, 77, 126

T

Target Stores, 9
Targeted, 33, 39, 55–58
Targeted emails, 55, 57
Teeth, 23
Telephone Sales, 83–85
Television, 47, 79, 81, 122
Television advertising, 79, 81
Testimonials, 76, 114, 135
Thanks, 1
Trade Shows, 28, 108, 117–119, 121
Trademarks, 66
Traditional, 2
Trumpet, 27
Tumblr, 11
TV, 43, 79, 81–82, 93
tweet, 138, 140
Twitter, 5, 35, 64, 138–141

U

Unique, 52, 77
University, 3, 203

V

Valuable content, 23, 25,
    32, 102, 112, 129
Vendors, 68, 108
Ventures, 115
Video, 8, 33, 64, 118,
    122–124, 132, 155,
    159–160, 173–174, 179
Viewers, 116, 129
Virtual, 8, 121
Visitors, 10, 15, 28
Visuals, 124
Vouchers, 120

W

Warranty, 116
Webinar, 10, 103–104, 119
Webinars, 102–103, 118,
    121
Welcome, 3, 42, 56
Window Signs, 99
Wonderful, 2
Wordpresss.org, 11
Worldwide, 1, 7–8, 10,
    33–34, 70

Y

Yellow Pages, 37, 68–69
Yelp, 32
YouTube, 34

Made in United States
Troutdale, OR
09/24/2023